LEABHARLANNA CHONTAE FHINE GALL
FINGAL COUNTY LIBRARIES

Items should be returned on or before the last date shown below. Items may be renewed by personal application, writing, telephone or by accessing the online Catalogue Service on Fingal Libraries' website. To renew give date due, borrower ticket number and PIN number if using online catalogue. Fines are charged on overdue items and will include postage incurred in recovery. Damage to, or loss of items will be charged to the borrower

Date Due	Date Due	Date Due
7/6/16		
26)4		
9/5		
24. JUL 18.		

RUNNING FULL CIRCLE

Footprints on a rocky
road to redemption

FRANK GREALLY

Ballpoint Press

This book is dedicated to Marian and our children:
Tomás, Catherine, Conor, Laura and Claire.

Running Full Circle is also dedicated to my brother, Tom;
to the memory of our parents, Tom and Kathleen Greally;
and to each and every person that I know who has been
kind to me in both calm and turbulent times.

Published in 2015 by Ballpoint Press
4 Wyndham Park, Bray, Co Wicklow, Republic of Ireland.
Telephone: 00353 86 821 7631
Email: ballpointpress1@gmail.com
Web: www.ballpointpress.ie

ISBN 978-0-9932892-6-2

Book production by Richard Gallagher and Joe Coyle

Cover design by The Design Gang

Cover photograph by Ray McManus, Sportsfile

Photograph layouts by Outburst Design

Printed and bound by GraphyCems

Contents

Acknowledgements

I OWE thanks to a good many people for their help and encouragement during the writing and production of this book.

First and always foremost, my wife, Marian, and our children — Tomás, Catherine, Conor, Laura and Claire — for their encouragement and patience.

The project was something I had toyed with for a few years, and but for the insistence of my great friend Ray McManus I might have continued to baulk.

The same goes for my publisher PJ Cunningham, himself a journalist and author, who persuaded me that the idea was not entirely madcap and expertly guided the process throughout.

My friend Gerry Duffy read early drafts and offered invaluable advice.

Thanks to colleagues at Athletics Ireland, especially CEO John Foley, for their continuing support and encouragement.

Peadar Staunton endured my dysfunctional editorial style back in the early years of *Irish Runner* magazine yet answered the call when I needed the best designer in the land to produce a cover.

Richard Gallagher, another *Irish Runner* veteran and a man who can spot a typo while minding mice at a crossroads in a gale, read the manuscript at various stages.

Thanks to old team-mates from the Irish Brigade in East Tennessee, in particular Ray McBride, Neil Cusack, Louis Kenny and Tom McCormack, who helped jog my recollection in the matter of half-remembered stories.

My brother, Tom, though far away in Australia, was my go-to man in recalling episodes, names and places from our childhood.

And for the inspiration and encouragement to write, thanks to three literary heroes, mentors and friends: the late, great and incomparable Con Houlihan, David McClellan and Jack Higgs.

Foreword

THIS is my story and the only story I have a right to tell. In telling it here as honestly as I can, I feel I have gone up on a high wire without any safety net.

I have come a long way since the day in 1970 I left home in Ballyhaunis on a meandering road that would take me to Dublin and then onward, but not always upward, to East Tennessee, USA.

There were many twist and turns and blind alleys on that road, and there have been times when along the way I felt desperately lost and alone. But somehow I always found some glimmer of hope that carried me through.

For too many years I was burdened with regret — regret for squandering running talents and educational opportunities. That regret became a millstone around my neck and I see now that it was a useless emotion.

Of course there are many things I wish I had done differently, but this was the path, at times chaotic, I chose and this is the only story I have to tell from the choices I made.

I know I have hurt people, including my dear wife, Marian, and wonderful children — Tomás, Catherine, Conor, Laura and Claire — but I believe writing this book has brought us closer as a family, and there have been smiles and tears as we shared parts of the manuscript.

We have experienced the pain of separation all too familiar in homes throughout Ireland, but we have never forgotten that in the end game it is family that matters most of all.

Similarly, differences with friends and colleagues have invariably given way to reconciliation, and whatever the rights or wrongs of such differences I take consolation from not having borne grudges or withheld the olive branch when there were chances to make up.

I am hugely fortunate to have met so many people of great and generous spirit, close friends and caring medical professionals, who have helped, sustained and inspired me through many crises and over many years.

I am just grateful now for the life I have, and the family and friends with whom I am still able to share that life, however topsy-turvy it has been, and for every bit of sweetness I have known along the way.

I have laid bare in these pages a little bit of my soul and some of what I have included has been painful to write. At the same time I have found healing in the process and would encourage others to keep even a private journal about their life experiences in as honest a way as possible

My chief hope is that this book may help even one person out there to believe that however stormy and dark the nights, hope and good friends can carry one through to a new day and a brighter horizon.

And if I have a single bit of advice for anyone reading my story it consists of just three words: Don't Give Up!

I suppose in the long run, what matters is not what I might have done, should have done, would have done, could have done. What matters is that what I did will leave a footprint, however small.

Life is a precious gift. Hold on and Don't Give Up!

1

Homeward Bound

WE were about an hour out of Shannon Airport on a September morning in 1976 when the dread of coming home fully kicked in — the waves of anxiety similar to what I had felt when travelling in the opposite direction, westward, heading from Ireland back to East Tennessee State University, where I had been pursuing a four-year athletics scholarship.

I always found it hard leaving home and have always believed home is wherever you originally start out from. My homeward journey on this occasion was taking me first to Shannon, then on to Dublin, then by train back to the small house in the village of Devlis, County Mayo, from where I had set out four years earlier.

You might imagine there would have been a spring in my step on that bright September morning as the Irish coastline swung into view. But no — the dominant emotion as I contemplated the final few legs of this final homecoming was the intuition of failure, the feeling I had squandered the rare and wonderful gift offered by those four years in the land of opportunity.

The truth is I would probably not have left Tennessee at all that year had my student visa not expired, and I would likely have maintained the cheerful tone of letters to my ageing parents — letters assuring them yet again how well I was doing as graduation neared. I would write those letters while humming a song that had become something of a mantra: 'Never tell the world your troubles/ Smiles are better far than tears/ Tell them you will be home soon/ Though you may be gone for years.'

I had found it desperately hard leaving great friends in Johnson City, a place in the East Tennessee hills that had become a home from home for me since I arrived there in the autumn of 1972. A handful of close friends had seen me from every angle over those four years and never judged or chided me when I careered off on wild and pitted paths far removed from the discipline and dedication demanded of a scholarship athlete.

My last year in Tennessee had been my toughest ever, and decades later I still marvel at how I survived it. The bright dreams of running success had all vanished, and those twelve months in Johnson City had become a grim matter of day-to-day survival, with no scholarship funds and only the kindness of true friends to rely on.

And still the letters home had remained resolutely upbeat, full of promise and expectation. I knew it had been heartbreaking for both my parents when I accepted the scholarship to ETSU; they had for some years relied on me to bring a little sunshine into their own challenging lives.

My only brother, Tom, then an Augustinian priest, was far away in Australia, and Dad's recurring bouts of depression had for long been a huge strain on Mam and himself. And so I had felt real guilt when leaving for the US — abandoning them, as it seemed, when they needed me most — but they had both been adamant I grab the opportunity and make the best of it.

The long descent into Shannon passed in a blur, and as we touched down on Irish tarmac the dreadful feeling of failure clung to me like a cold, wet blanket. My American dream had turned into a nightmare and I would soon be walking up the front path in Devlis with little or nothing to show for my years away.

During the short stopover in Shannon I phoned my good friend Neil Cusack — a fellow student at ETSU, winner of the Boston Marathon in 1974, and the man who had helped recruit me to the team that became known on the collegiate running circuit as The Irish Brigade.

Neil, more than anyone, knew how things had panned out for me, especially in that final year in Johnson City. He had seen me compete with reasonable success for my first two years in college and had also witnessed my subsequent decline and burnout.

The voice at the other end of the phone that September morning was as concerned and supportive as ever; sensing a crisis and taking charge of the situation, Neil instructed me to take the passenger exit from Shannon and spend a few days with him before the onward journey.

'I'd love nothing better,' I told him, 'but my bags are checked through to Dublin.'

'That's not a problem,' he said. 'I know a lad working in Shannon — I'll ask him to get your bags sorted out in Dublin and we can drive up there and collect them tomorrow. Give me ten minutes and call me back.'

It was an idea straight from left field, but it brought a deep sense of relief. Ten minutes later I was back on the phone to find that everything had indeed been arranged: Neil's contact knew a man who knew another man who would pick my bags off the carousel in Dublin and stash them till we got there.

Minutes later Neil arrived to pick me up. As I got into the car he assured me that after a few days with him in Limerick I would be restored and ready to face the last few laps of my journey to Mayo, Ballyhaunis and Devlis.

2

Bags And Baggage

HOW simple it was back in 1976! That you could disembark a plane in Shannon in the knowledge that when it landed in Dublin your bags would be identified and stored awaiting pick-up. It would hardly happen today. It was huge relief to see Neil Cusack's smiling face. He exuded positivity and good humour — just what I needed to lift my flagging spirits that September morning — and soon we were on the road to Dublin. It felt a bit crazy, driving a round trip 250 miles to salvage a few books and shirts and shoes and a toothbrush, but it was also blessed relief to chat and laugh with a pal who had empathy for where I was at in my head at that time.

True to his word, Neil's associate at the airport had shepherded my bags to a safe place, and soon we were back down the road to Limerick, the pair of us in high glee, remembering good times in Tennessee and delighting in the mad impulse that had brought us on this cross-country odyssey to rescue my humble chattels.

The few days in Limerick brought sweet respite and allowed me get set in my head for the fateful final miles to Mayo and home. Days of good food cooked by Neil's mother, Tess, and nights of lively conversation into the wee hours, the obligatory bottle of beer or two no hindrance. The warm bed and the morning lie-on were balm to my troubled spirit, but there remained a deep unease about facing the folks at home.

My original journey to Tennessee had been triggered by a meeting with Neil in Cambridge, England, four years previously when we were both members of the Ireland team at the International Cross Country Championships.

I was just 20 at the time and my running profile had grown rapidly in the two years since my arrival in Dublin to work and join Donore Harriers, the club in Islandbridge that was then the powerhouse of Irish distance running.

The legendary Eddie Hogan was the head coach at Donore and it was under his guidance that I made spectacular progress. In August 1970 I set a national junior record, 30 minutes and 17 seconds, for 10,000m in Santry — leading from the front with the fearlessness of youth and beating a strong field of elite seniors.

Two years later I made the Irish senior team for what is now known as the World Cross Country Championships, and it was in Cambridge at the time that Neil enquired if I would consider a scholarship to ETSU, where he was already a star.

The idea of a US scholarship was what might nowadays be called a no-brainer. I was delivering the post in Fingal, working out of Swords, and the heady thoughts of running and training in the mountains of East Tennessee, as described by Neil, seemed much more exciting than the daily struggle with illegible handwriting and inscrutable dogs.

My schooling had come to an abrupt halt when after four years in St Patrick's College Ballyhaunis I decided, much to the consternation of my parents, that I had enough of formal learning.

The only subject that held my attention was English literature, and I read widely and voraciously. Already I had some vague ambitions to write, but I was overwhelmed with anxiety as I contemplated facing my final year in St Patrick's and the dreaded Leaving Cert.

And so I quit formal education and was blessed to immediately land a job as a junior postman in Ballyhaunis, where I greatly enjoyed a couple of years delivering telegrams around the countryside and when not on telegram duty spending leisurely hours in the upstairs room of the post office immersed in a book as I explored the wide and wonderful world of great literature.

It was only when I turned 17 that I discovered a talent for running — though I had taken my first, faltering strides much earlier.

3

Around The Road

I BELIEVE it was my grandfather on my mother's side, Harry Mannion, who first sowed the seed that eventually brought me to athletics and in particular distance running.

As a boy of six or seven, I loved to hear grandfather tell the story of a day when he walked the long journey to an outlying village sports and won the 100-yard and 220-yard races. He would regale me with how he rose on that Sunday morning and milked the cows and did all the other farm chores before setting out on the ten-mile hike, carrying with him a five-naggin bottle of buttermilk and a cake of wholemeal bread baked by himself.

I would listen enthralled, seeing in my mind's eye the *boreens* travelled, the crowds in the village sportsfield, the smell of the crushed grass, the flailing runners, and every yard of the races he won. And then I would pester him to repeat the story over and over again. Eventually I found myself lining up for the 100 yards, under eight, at the Annual Abbey Pattern. I was a bag of nerves, desperately wanting to win so I could tell grandfather about my success.

I got a great start and for the first 50 yards was running on air — in full flight and going for glory. Then my skinny, bare feet began to lose traction and soon I was travelling in slow motion, running on the spot as the others swept past.

I had tried too hard to achieve success, and it was an early lesson I am still not sure I have ever fully grasped or learned.

Pat Cribbin it was who eventually persuaded me to take up distance running for sport. Years later, I still see my dear friend

— long since departed — running by our house in the early morning on his way to work in the joinery, a pint bottle of milk sticking out of one pocket of his heavy work coat and a wrapped lunch poking out of the other.

Big Pat had read that the legendary Olympic champion Emil Zatopek trained in heavy boots, and so the boots he wore on those morning runs long ago were sturdy enough to help absorb the impact of his six-foot-plus frame on the tarmac.

Pat would call in to our house most evenings on his way home from work and hold forth, sometimes for hours, on his favourite sports: boxing and running. Back in those days Pat was a mould breaker and sports fanatic — and one of the closest friends I ever had.

We were 17, and football on a Sunday had been my only competitive outlet until one evening Pat invited me to join him on a run around a two-mile lap that skirted the nearby village of Lecarrow, where he lived.

That first night I managed to run half a mile before stopping for breath, after which Pat, the original meet-and-train motivator, coaxed and cajoled me the rest of the way. Little did I suspect as I staggered to the finish that night that for decades to come running would in one form or another be central to my life.

Soon after that first run, Pat encouraged me to join the local boxing club, which had been revived by Mick Nestor, our go-to barber in Ballyhaunis. I did not prove to be a great scrapper, but I enjoyed the roadwork, when a group of us would run about three miles.

For weeks too after that maiden voyage on Pat's favourite circuit, which he always referred to as 'around the road', I joined my pal on his nightly run — his morning run to work was only a warm-up according to his training schedule.

Soon I could run the full circuit without stopping. To me that was a breakthrough; to Pat it was small apples, because most nights he ran three circuits.

We surely looked an odd couple in those days of the late 1960s — both in heavy sweaters, loose-fitting trousers and army boots, and myself, all of seven stone, trying gamely to match strides with the giant.

Of course some people concluded we were more than a little touched — at least one concerned neighbour warned my mother I would strain my heart — but by now I was hooked on running, and waiting at six most mornings for the low whistle from Pat that signalled it was time to hit the road for the first training run of the day.

I had made rapid progress and I loved those bracing pre-breakfast runs regardless of what the neighbours might think.

Soon Pat and I began to look the part, having made a shopping trip to the metropolis (Galway City) for tracksuits and running shoes. We even formed a club — and to prove it was really a club, another great friend, Michael Joyce, signed up.

The three of us read obsessively about running. I took a subscription to *Athletics Weekly* and every Sunday morning would present myself at the postal sorting office to claim my little bible of athletics from the clerk on duty.

At last came the day of our first race: a cross-country run on Tuam Racecourse. Fired by the impetuosity that would cost me in many a subsequent race, I set off like a very startled hare — and by halfway was watching from the ditch as Eddie Leddy of Ballinamore powered to victory. I little thought then that within a few years I would be joining the winner as a fellow student and running team-mate in East Tennessee.

Of course I persevered after that disastrous debut — Pat would have had it no other way — and a few weeks later, at the Mayo cross-country championships in Hollymount, our little club team won its first medals. What joy!

A few hours before that race we were still one man short of a full team, and staring at more disappointment, when Pat said he had heard mention of a young fellow who was by all accounts the fittest lad ever to kick a football in the county of Roscommon. And so in Mick Nestor's untrusty Ford Consul we headed across the county border to Ballinlough in search of our anchorman.

At their farmstead in the townland of Coolcrim, Padraig Keane's parents didn't quite welcome us with open arms — there were chores to be done and this rough and unready crew were shaping to spirit their young lad to distant Hollymount on some frivolous pursuit. Fortunately, diplomacy won the day, our team numbers saw a 25 percent increase — and for good measure Padraig finished second in the race.

I doubt if anyone in Hollymount that day imagined that within a few years young Keane and young Greally would be running for Ireland, and on the senior team too. But it did happen, and when it did there was no prouder man than Pat Cribbin.

Padraig Keane went on to achieve greatness in athletics. He ran for Ireland many times and for years after moving to Dublin was the lynchpin of Clonliffe Harriers' cross-country and road-relay teams.

For a while Ballyhaunis Athletic Club enjoyed great success. But too soon our little group scattered. Padraig and I emigrated to Dublin; Pat took the boat to Holyhead and the train to Birmingham.

Pat kept in touch, his letters vividly describing awesome training sessions at his adopted club, Birchfield Harriers, where another of our heroes, Ian Stewart, was a member.

Then one morning in Tennessee a letter arrived from home with the news that Pat had been killed in a road accident on his way to work.

Years later, there is hardly a day goes by that in some context or other I don't think of my dear comrade. He was on my mind too the morning in 1976 when I shook hands with my good friend Neil Cusack and left Limerick for the last leg of my homeward journey from Tennessee.

4

Light In The Tunnel

THEY were innocent times, those years when I attempted to grow up in Ballyhaunis. I believe I laid a good foundation for later running exploits when, for four-odd years from the age of 12, I spent most Sundays in season with a group loosely termed The Hunters, tramping for miles over hills and hollows on the trail of hares and foxes.

Our whipper-in was Jim Moylett, who had earned a big reputation as a champion boxer at home and in the USA and was still a very fit man, passionate about hunting with his beloved greyhounds. And each Sunday of the hunt our motley group would gather around Jim after first Mass in the Augustinian Friary to learn our intended starting point and plan of campaign.

We youngsters would trek for miles with Jim and his group of experienced hunters. Sometimes we might join up with the local gun club and help 'beat out' foxes from cover.

I was also very active helping my father with chores on the Friary Farm, where he worked for several years after the building industry went into decline.

My father was a plasterer by trade and a perfectionist for good measure. He loved his work on the buildings and had a proud reputation for high standards. I think it broke his heart when the work dried up and he had to find other ways to put bread on the table.

I loved the Augustinian farm, and from the age of 15 gave many hours working there, often milking the four cows twice a day and doing whatever other jobs were needed. There were days back then when I had to stand in full-time for my father, days when anxiety and depression so crippled him he could hardly get out of bed.

I had no understanding then of what ailed him — I simply filled in, doing the morning and evening chores and relishing the challenge. It was only much later that I came to learn the hard way about anxiety and depression and had to fight my own long battle with both foes. That experience would help me much better understand my late father and love him even more.

I searched for some bit of light relief for the final few miles of my homeward journey, and it was a memory of Michael Joyce, the first pal I made on my very first day at school, that brought a smile.

I thought of a dark winter night when Michael, Pat Cribbin and myself were clipping it out 'around the road'. For some reason, Michael was feeling especially frisky and had raced ahead, disappearing from sight and sound around the winding boreen, with big Pat and myself in cold pursuit.

Suddenly, the silence was rent by a blood-curdling scream, mingled with a deep roar that could only be bestial in origin — and almost immediately Michael emerged from the gloom, hurtling toward us like the proverbial bat out of hell.

When he eventually stopped running and regained some composure he told the breathless tale. He had just started congratulating himself for stealing a march on Pat and myself when he ran full tilt into some monstrous creature, hairy, hot and smelly. Worse still, the stray donkey — for such it proved to be — let out an unearthly roar as the terrified Michael recoiled and fled for safety.

We had often laughed about that incident, as we did about another little Michael Joyce gem from those salad days in Mayo.

It was dark and eerie of a November morning as Michael ran through Devlis to join me for a pre-dawn training session. Dressed in white — from beanie to top to gloves to leggings to shoes — he loped past the Wall homestead, unaware that Frank Wall, the man of the house, had died suddenly during the night.

As he sped by, he caught a fleeting glance of a small group of women making their way to early Mass in the Friary, but he pushed on silently, head down, offering no greeting.

Later that day, while buying a newspaper in Waldron's shop in Abbey Street, he overheard Mrs Waldron lament the sudden passing of her close neighbour. And then came the startling revelation.

'And do you know something?' she said, her voice dropping to a reverential whisper. 'Mrs Toolin saw poor Frank's ghost this morning, on her way to first Mass!'

5

Plastering The Cracks

MY mother was wonderfully warm and caring, but she didn't mince her disapproval, especially if I had fallen short in some task about the house or garden. My father was similarly forthright.

'Glory be to God Almighty!' he would call out to my mother. 'Come out here quick and see the mess this fellow is after making of cutting the hedge!'

From an early age, I sensed why my brother, Tom, sought out the sanctuary of the Friary, doing odd jobs there during summer holidays from Saint Jarlath's.

It wasn't as if my parents set out to criticise; I believe they were two very frustrated people to whom life had dealt an unfair share of bad cards. There was always some financial stress floating around, especially in the years my father worked as a plasterer for his brother-in-law. That was a strange alliance that seemed to increase rather than ease the sense of insecurity at home.

Many a bright summer morning my father would leave the house to walk the mile or so across the fields to the brother-in-law's. He would have the brown lunchbox in the crook of an arm and his mood would be upbeat. I would watch him walk across those fields until he went out of sight and I would stay looking out the upstairs window, hoping and praying I would not see him at any moment reappear.

'Is there any sign of him?' my mother would nervously call from downstairs after about half an hour had elapsed.

'No, I think it must be okay,' was the response I always hoped to make, but all too often I would have to deliver the unwanted news

— that even though the day was perfect for outdoor work father would be doing no plastering, because there he was coming back home, this time without the spring in his step.

Even then I could not understand why he tolerated what seemed abuse from his brother-in-law, a man who held himself in high esteem in the community but might decide on a whim, on any given day, to send his small crew back home before they started.

It depended not on whether there was work to be done — there usually was — but simply on the boss's mood, and of course each day without work was also a day without pay, something that greatly increased the anxiety in our household and heightened the tension between my parents.

My father would arrive back home on those sunny summer mornings and I would hear my mother implore him to leave the brother-in-law and strike out on his own as a contractor or at least find some decent employer who would treat him with respect. My father was widely known for his plastering skills, a fact of which my mother often reminded him. As she put it, 'You are blocking your own light.'

Many years after he left the building trade, I would still get locals pointing out to me and admiring jobs he had done around our town.

'You would have made a fortune if you had listened to me,' my mother would often tell him — as if he needed to be told.

Other days my father would arrive home and, to the delight of my mother, inform us he had told the brother-in-law where to stick his job. There would be jubilation for a few hours after that announcement and the tension and worry would seem to subside.

Then Aunt Mary, my father's sister, would arrive to plead with him to change his mind. She would have been sent on this errand by her husband, and I believe the reason my father never had the heart to tell her no was because he and she had an exceptionally close bond.

And yet this small-time building contractor presented himself as a pillar of society, driving a nice car and never missing his annual pilgrimage to the Galway Races. It was hard to believe he could make money, especially with all those cancelled work days, but he kept up all the appearances of a wealthy man while those who toiled faithfully for him were left to stress and worry.

One thing that kept bread on our table during that time was a bit of part-time farming. My parents rented fields across the road from our house and there they raised cattle and sheep and grew potatoes and vegetables.

Before their marriage, my father and mother had been next-door neighbours in the village of Drimbane, about a mile from Ballyhaunis.

My mother experienced trauma at age 13 when her own mother died and she effectively had to fill her shoes. A brother and sister, Michael and Eileen, left home to find work and it was she who was there for her father all the days of his life from when his wife died to his own passing many years later in his early 90s.

Harry Mannion had a great appreciation of good literature and music and had a well stocked library in his home, the first house in the village. He raised the family by the fruits of his labour on his small but meticulously kept farm. He was a learned man and encouraged me from an early age to read the classics of literature — and of course he also ignited my interest in athletics.

I never knew my father's parents, but I got on well with his two brothers and their children, who all lived in Drimbane. I spent many happy days in that same village when life seemed very simple indeed.

Crushed Tenderness

I THINK my father's spirit remained firmly rooted in the village of Drimbane, where he and my mother had grown up. I believe his hope was that he and my mother would end up moving back to the house at the head of the road into the village, my maternal grandfather's, where they had lived till my brother was seven.

There were, however, tensions between the Mannion and Greally families, and I never found out the exact causes of those tensions.

Grandfather Harry Mannion was a man of great principle and culture. His wife had been a schoolteacher, and when she died tragically young he became fiercely protective of his brood.

In the years that my mother and Tom lived with Grandfather, my father worked in England. That was during the second World War, when work was scarce at home and skilled tradesmen were taking the boat to Holyhead and the onward train to London, Manchester or Birmingham.

My father ended up in London and like so many of his generation sent back money every week by telegram. He would come home at Christmas, but would stay at his own parents' house, where my mother and brother would visit him.

It was, to say the least, a strange arrangement — and given they had not seen each other in 12 months and were about to face another 12 months apart, I can only imagine how the three of them must have suffered. They all three paid a heavy price for my grandfather's high principles.

I'm sure my mother hoped that her father's opposition to her husband would soften in time and that she and my father might end up running the small farm and living together in her childhood home. But that is not the way things worked out.

Harry Mannion had one son, Michael, who had gone away to carve a career for himself in the retail business and was happily employed managing a shop in Ballina. Michael — or Uncle Miko, as we referred to him — had shown little or no interest in farming while growing up, but in 1949 he was summoned home by his father to take over the farm, which was no more than 25 acres.

He made a reluctant return, and his arrival meant my mother and brother had to find a new place to live. That was how things were done back then; the eldest son had first refusal on the inheritance. But it was with a heavy heart that Michael Mannion arrived back home to take up the role of farmer, an occupation in which he was never to feel comfortable.

Years later, when Grandfather had passed on, Uncle Miko ended up selling most of the little holding. He became, as my mother would have put it, 'a bit too fond of drink' and in his later years struck a lonely figure when arriving under the weather at our house for Sunday dinner.

Michael always regretted returning to the farm in Drimbane and eventually found whatever solace he could in alcohol. There was a deep core loneliness about my uncle that I found hard to understand when growing up — but I would eventually, through personal and bitter experience, learn much of anxiety, loneliness and alcohol.

Boy Behind The Wires

MY couple of years working as a junior postman in Ballyhaunis will always have a special place in my memory. I had dropped out of formal schooling and sat a test for the position on a day when there were just two of us in the examination room: myself and a son of my mother's best friend.

I managed to get the best marks and, after a medical examination, was deemed suitable to be splendidly decked out in a new uniform and assigned a shiny bicycle complete with three-speed gears.

Those were peak years for telegrams, the late Sixties. The busiest days were Thursday and Friday as money orders arrived from Britain, and I would be in full flight delivering good news and welcome income to families in the townlands and villages dotted to north, south, east and west of our town. These families might have a father, son or daughter working in England, Wales or Scotland, and every week, without fail, the money would arrive by telegram to Ballyhaunis Post Office.

The downside of the job was having to deliver bad news — telegrams bringing tidings of a sudden death were always hard to deal with; the gears would grind much more slowly when I knew the message I had on board was a sad one.

I soon knew every village within a wide radius of the Post Office and I came to know almost every family living in those villages. It was a time of lovely innocence when all I needed to do was ride my trusty machine — whistling and singing as I sped along my merry way.

Johnny Henry, chief clerk in Ballyhaunis Post Office, had a

couple of titles for me. The Wire Boy was one and the Boy Messenger was another. On a busy Friday, with the Post Office packed to the door, Johnny could be heard shouting up the chute whence the telegrams were dispatched from the telephonist's upstairs office.

'Send down the Wire Boy!' was the order aloft to Myra Fitzgerald, and I would duly arrive down to the front counter to be greeted by a gaggle of convent schoolgirls queueing for stamps.

'Make way for the Wire Boy!' one or more of them would cry, and as the giggles erupted I wished the ground would open up and swallow me.

It had been bad enough to be nicknamed The Mouse Greally in National School because I was small and puny for my age.

That Mouse moniker had followed me around town for a good while, but then an incident occurred that rendered it obsolete, at least in my mind.

For months I had dreaded the walk to school, because every morning as I approached Lisheen, a bump in the road, I would meet a certain Tommy on his way to work for a farmer up the road.

Tommy was about 14 and the ritual was always the same; he would block my path and push me around, often with a few thumps and kicks to drive home whatever point he was trying to prove. When he had satisfied his perverse urge, he would continue on his way laughing loudly as he lit a cigarette.

It was bad enough to be heading for a classroom where fear ruled, but Tommy's approach made me sick to the pit of my stomach because I always knew what was coming.

Then one morning I snapped — kicking him in the shins with all my force and following up with a mighty punch that hit him flush on the nose.

I was only a puny thing but I made a powerful impact on big Tommy, who roared in pain and hopped around on one leg while trying to stem the blood pumping from his nose.

I felt great satisfaction that morning, and Tommy never

bothered me again — except for the few expletives thrown my way as we passed on the road. I was doubly pleased when word of the giant-killing reached the school-yard courtesy of several kids who had witnessed it.

I rarely got into fights in school, but whenever I subsequently did, bolstered by that showdown, I held my ground — like the mouse that roared.

If those college girls were giving me a hard time and messing with my self-image during my 'wire boy' days, Mick Nestor — our athletics mentor, motivator and transport manager — was a great man to rebuild confidence, and most mornings I started off my working day with a stroll round the town and a visit to his barber shop in The Square.

Mick was an eternal optimist, a lively and engaging character who was regarded by some in Ballyhaunis as a 'blow-in'. Within a few months of his arrival he had set up as a barber and revived the boxing club that years earlier enjoyed much success, even hosting an international tournament in the Friary Field.

From our first meeting, when I turned up for sparring practice, Mick seemed to believe in me. He soon figured I was unlikely to make a World or even a Mayo boxing champion, but right from the start he maintained I had the talent to become a distance runner worthy of the name.

I'd sit in the big chair and Mick, the eternal optimist, would playfully spin me around while talking big dreams.

'You have a great little fighting spirit,' he'd say. 'I can see you going all the way to the Olympics.'

On leaving Mick's shop I would wander up the town, stopping at Webb's the butchers and Pat Keane's the cobblers before heading farther up Main Street to Rita Flatley in the newsagents. Then I'd cross the road to Michael 'Ronnie' Curley in the Medical Hall before returning to the Post Office and my room with a view onto Bridge Street.

One market day I looked out the window and was witness to a

fist fight between two very grown men. It seemed one of the protagonists had been a ganger on a County Council road crew and the other had been a member of that crew but a notorious malingerer.

As the two confronted each other, I heard the ganger offer the jibe: 'I see you're not hiding under the bush today.'

That was enough to spark an intense and dramatic bout of fisticuffs on the rain-sodden street that was as good a piece of action — because so close to home and in real-life technicolour — as any I had seen in westerns at the Parochial Hall.

I loved those idle moments looking out that first-floor window, observing the comings and goings of townsfolk and village folk in the street below, their quirks and mannerisms, watching small human dramas unfold — and all the time dreaming the big dreams Mick the Barber had been spinning for me as I spun round in the big chair.

Had I had not gone the postal route and become the Wire Boy, I might well have ended up riding thoroughbreds at the Galway Races in Ballybrit.

Rose, a lovely mare belonging to Joe Horkan, used to help me draw home cocks of hay at the Friary Farm, where my father worked, and on those summer evenings, riding bareback, I would feel at one with Rose as we galloped along.

Mick Webb, who owned the meat factory in Ballyhaunis, urged my parents more than once to send me to his friend the great Tom Dreaper, of Arkle fame, in County Meath, to try out as an apprentice.

Mick even called me 'Dreaper': 'I can see you have a way with horses, young Dreaper. For God's sake, get your parents to understand that you have the makings of a great little jockey.'

Despite Mick's repeated pleadings, my mother refused point plank; horseriding, she ruled, was far too dangerous an occupation. Had she suspected the dangers I would face as a competitive athlete she might have relented.

8

Boys Of Derrydonnell

THE pungent aroma of wintergreen always evokes for me summer evenings in the late 1960s and dressing-rooms in far-flung villages and towns of Connacht. The familiar smell would greet you before you reached the door as runners inside lathered hamstrings, calves and even elbows with the 'magic rub'.

There was always a great air of expectation and excitement in those dressing-rooms — male-only domains in an era before women became part of the rich fabric of the road-running circuit.

Often the town or village in question was hosting its Summer Festival — a week-long celebration of music and dance and carnival fun — and a group of us from Ballyhaunis would land to stage a raid on the midweek Festival Road Race.

The hometown festival was a time when emigrants took a couple of weeks' respite from the building sites of London and Manchester and the factories of Coventry to come home and drink porter and regale family and friends with tall tales of rough and rowdy days working with McAlpine and Murphy and Wimpy.

These young and not so young emigrants brought back for the duration some light relief and even some colour to the small towns and villages of Mayo, but the downside followed when the fun ended with tearful partings on rail platforms at Westport, Castlebar, Claremorris and Ballyhaunis, when the whistle down the track as the train approached was the lonesome summons that caused many strong men and even stronger women to break down.

I was one of those who stayed in Ireland until a US scholarship beckoned, and it was in those small towns that I learned something of the craft of road racing from such hardy perennials as Willie Morris, Tommy Madden and Kevin Ryan — mighty men of Derrydonnell Athletic Club who put their own stamp on Irish distance running.

In Ballyhaunis AC we always wondered if the Derrydonnell men would show up for our road race, because the arrival of their minibus virtual guaranteed the destiny of the main prizes.

They were rugged but friendly characters who never failed to encourage us youngsters. We looked on them as professionals — teak-tough men who arrived looking fabulously fit and gave no quarter in the heat of battle. Stories circulated about their savage training runs in Connemara. That they had their own bus added to the mystique.

I often travelled to road races with runners from Tuam AC, another group of seasoned campaigners that included Tom Flanagan, Roger Rushe, Mickey Kelly and Tom Lardner.

I was a young runner full of passion and enthusiasm, blissfully unaware of the need to learn about pacing, sprinting flat out from the gun. Long before I was up to it, I would try to match strides with Madden and Ryan and Sean Reilly and Brendan Mooney.

Holding on grimly in the closing miles of those early races, in maybe fifth or sixth position, it happened more than once that from behind came the steady and relentless patter of feet, the feet of the veteran Willie Morris pacing himself to perfection in the heel of the hunt and snatching priceless team points for Derrydonnell.

After a race from Easkey to Dromore West in Sligo, Willie — by then about 50 but still a sprightly and shrewd campaigner and a legend out west — approached me and bestowed a nugget of wisdom: 'You're a great little runner and you have great heart, but you must learn how to pace yourself and run your own race.'

It was a lesson that I never forgot but didn't always obey.

And then there came days when I was able to match and even beat the great men of Derrydonnell — in those heady days they were delighted I had learned my trade well. My mentor Willie Morris was especially pleased and told me so.

Noel Henry was another great mentor and supporter and, like Willie Morris, had an uncanny sense of pace that helped earn him a national marathon title. He was also a pioneer of ultra-distance running and had lovely running form on road and track.

Ronnie Long was another early influence and often went miles out of his way driving me to and from sports and road races. I learned much from running those evening road races and have fond memories of victories in the likes of Kiltimagh, Claremorris and Westport. I was also showing good track form, especially over three miles and 5,000 metres, distances at which I notched up Mayo and Connacht titles.

There were great Open Sports in those days and almost every summer Sunday would find me hitching to places like Mayo Abbey, Ballyglass, Aughagower and Newport. It could be well after midnight when I made it home, often laden down with cups and medals.

There were days I travelled to village sports with Joe Freely, a talented sprinter from Ballyhaunis who had made a name for himself in schools competitions — he was a boarder at Gormanston College, County Meath. Joe and his father, Mike, and myself enjoyed some great days on track and road and always returned home with prizes.

Those sports were my proving ground and great preparation for when I moved to Dublin and joined Donore Harriers.

I was always a bag of nerves before races, but once the gun went the nerves vanished. I was a front runner and it never mattered how good the opposition was — I just took off, putting everyone under pressure, including of course myself.

It was the same when I attended training organised by Padraig Griffin, coach to the Leddy Brothers, PJ and Eddie. Padraig was ahead of his time, and he and kindred pioneers such as Murt Hynes and Liam Kavanagh organised brilliant training weekends in Galway.

Even though still a junior learning the trade on those weekends, I would challenge senior elites like Tom O'Riordan, Mattie Murphy, Fr Paddy Coyle, Eddie Spillane and Jim McNamara on the Sunday morning long run. I knew no other way but running from the front.

I made a trip to Dublin during those early years to sign up for what was known as the BLE Summer School on the grounds of UCD Belfield. I stayed in a B&B in the city centre and each morning got the bus to Belfield, and it was there I met Jack Sweeney, an early coach to Ronnie Delany.

Jack took me under his wing but could not understand why I did not want to learn about field events or hurdles, all part of the week-long curriculum.

'I only came here to learn more about running and that's all I'm going to do,' I told him.

It was at the same Summer School that I first got to train with Eddie and PJ Leddy. It was a big deal for me to get to train with two of my special heroes, and I could not wait to get back home and share the experience with Michael Joyce and Pat Cribbin.

Dublin City was strange and wonderful to me, but after a few days away I was keen to return to Ballyhaunis and put what I had learned about distance running into practice. I was living and breathing athletics at the time. How I wish that innocent passion had lasted longer than it did!

9

Local Heroes

THE 1968 Olympic 10,000m final made a lasting impression on me. I watched the race in Morley's pub with Padraig Keane, Michael Joyce and our mentor Mick Nestor, and it was brilliant to see some of my heroes in action, especially Ron Hill, whose exploits I had been reading about in *Athletics Weekly*.

Hill was a runner's runner who personified what a good clubman should be and was high on my list of role models. But I had local heroes in Ballyhaunis too, and not all of them were runners. I was especially impressed by Tom Fitzgerald, a star of the Mayo Football Minors, and Michael 'Ronnie' Curley, who was reputed to have been a great sprinter in his day.

Tom Fitzgerald was a super-fit young man who trained hard and exuded energy and sense of purpose, and I loved to talk with him about strength and endurance and how to develop explosive speed.

The Fitzgerald family shop on Main Street was a regular port of call for me, as was 'Ronnie' Curley's place farther up Main Street. In those days when I worked as a Junior Postman I had lots of time to play with as I waited for the next telegram to arrive for delivery. I could wander up and down the town several times a day, and there was no pressure as long as I made regular check-back visits to the post office in Abbey Street.

Although Ronnie had been christened Michael, I rarely heard him called anything but Ronnie. During his years as a top-class sprinter he became known as Ronnie the Runner, a title of honour to be spoken in the same breath and with the same reverence reserved for the Olympic 1500-metre champion Ronnie Delany.

Ronnie Curley was still passionate about athletics even though his track career was by then well over. He gave me my first running spikes, a lovely, snug-fitting pair with green leather uppers that had been gathering dust in his attic. When I laced on those spikes up in the GAA Park on the Claremorris Road I was in another world.

I'd watch Tom Fitzgerald go through an intensive session before launching into my own routine, which usually consisted of a lengthy warm-up followed by interval laps of the pitch. I had read that Emil Zatopek used to complete 40 times 400 metres in a single session, and when doing intervals I often imagined I was the Czech legend. I'd finish off with half a dozen 100-yard sprints followed by several slow laps of the field to warm down.

In those idyllic years I would usually have a few training miles logged before work, and at lunchtime I would cycle home and spend half an hour running through the fields close to our house or sprinting up and down John Hunt's Hill across the road.

Three days a week I would be back out on the road in the evening for a third session. I training 'only' twice on the other days.

On Sunday mornings my good friend Padraig Keane, already five miles into his run, would swing by our house and I would join him for another 10 miles on the road. I loved those long runs with Padraig, not least for the curious looks on people's faces and their comments as we passed.

Padraig had made great strides since the day we spirited him away from chores on the family farm, and we had become firm friends but also fierce rivals on road, track and country.

On those Sunday-morning runs we talked about our heroes: Emil Zatopek, Ron Clarke, Ron Hill, Dave Bedford, Ian Stewart and Ian McCafferty — the men we read about in *Athletics Weekly*. We also had home-grown heroes, among them Mick Molloy of Oughterard, who finished the marathon at the Mexico Olympics in his bare feet.

Sean Reilly from Hollymount was another who inspired us; he

was the number one distance runner in Mayo and his career highlights included a great season in 1966 when he won Connacht junior and senior mile titles. For good measure he was an unassuming champion who was always encouraging to us newcomers.

The town of Hollymount was a lucky racing venue for me. It was my first proving ground when I was part of the little team from Ballyhaunis AC that medalled in the Mayo Junior Cross Country Championships, and I have fond memories of winning Mayo and Connacht cross-country titles in Gill's Field, where the going was usually what we called 'slightly swampy' and long spikes were the footwear of choice.

And then all of 50 years ago Sean Reilly and his brother Tom decided to expand the Mayo athletic scene, and so was born the Hollymount International Road Race in a town of maybe 250 souls.

I came close to winning the race in 1970 when Eddie Leddy — later to be a team-mate at ETSU — was almost hit by a passing car as I hunted him down. I thought my hour of immortality had arrived, forgetting it would take more than a reckless motorist to faze the surefooted Ballinamore man. Still, that runner-up spot remains a gem in the memory bank.

Of course we are talking about a time of innocence that now seems like another world. Sometimes to cheer myself up I recall a story told by Sean that I feel captures the essence of the era.

At the zenith of his career Sean had travelled to a village sports at the far end of Mayo, a pillion passenger on the Honda 50 of his friend Seamus Brannick. Arriving home after an exhausting but successful day, young Reilly found to his dismay that the house was silent and the fire was cold in the grate. His parents had gone visiting.

'I was ravenous with hunger and there was nothing ready to eat,' Sean told me years later. Starvation threatened but Sean's resourcefulness saved him.

'I did a quick search and found a grand piece of sirloin steak.

I was so hungry that for convenience and a quick result I just boiled the steak in the electric kettle — and to tell the truth a steak never tasted as good before or since.'

10

The Cup That Cheered

THE Quinlan Cup in Tullamore was a great proving ground for me and I have fond memories of what used to be Ireland's premier road race back in the late sixties and early seventies.

I was a callow 18 when I first ran the senior race, over six miles, but managed to finish in the top 20 and was delighted when the great Paddy Larkin of the organising club, Tullamore Harriers, offered a handshake and words of congratulation.

In those days the Quinlan Cup attracted the cream of distance running, was eagerly anticipated and got generous column inches — previews as well as reviews — in the national papers. Those were the days when Tom O'Riordan's twice-weekly columns in the *Irish Independent* were compulsory reading for us aspiring athletes in the wilds of Mayo.

Back in Ballyhaunis we even kept old newspapers so we could revisit accounts of Quinlan Cup epics from previous years. We read of men like Paddy Coyle, Mattie Murphy, Jim Timoney, O'Riordan himself, Mick Hayden, John Buckley, Donie Walsh, Dick Hodgins, Des McGann and Jim McNamara. And we dreamt of the day we would toe the line in the Midlands mecca.

And when for me that day did arrive, I was a bundle of nervous excitement as we lined up on the wide and handsome start area at the top of the town.

I had arrived early to get glimpses of my heroes and was not disappointed. Many of the big names were engaged in their pre-race rituals. Everyone I talked to warned me about the need to get out fast before the course narrowed after 400 metres and hurtled abruptly left over the bridge. That news in itself was enough to get the pulse soaring.

I did get out fast — right on the heels of the early leaders — and once the nerves settled I greatly enjoyed my first Quinlan Cup, not least for the enthusiastic and plentiful support around the course.

Just when I thought the end must be nigh, the great Willie Dunne moved alongside and I plucked up the courage to ask how far it might be to the finish. I was shocked when the 1960 Olympian told me we had a mile still to run.

I'm afraid the wily Donore man overstated matters by 600 yards. I doubt if I could have run another mile, and fortunately I didn't have to; the finish loomed up and I had survived the baptism of fire.

A highlight of that day was the huge array of prizes on display at the finish. Paddy Larkin's stamp was all over the post-race proceedings, though I did not realise at the time just how big an influence he was.

I returned to run the Quinlan Cup once more, in 1971 — by which time I had moved to Dublin and joined Donore Harriers — and my seventh-place finish in the senior race remains a treasured memory.

All runners have days when they are 'on fire', and that was such a day for me. I warmed up by jogging the three-mile lap, then throwing in a few sprints and stretches. I got a good spot on the starting grid and was away fast and in a big hurry too.

Finishing seventh in Tullamore was a great result for a junior. It brought me a bit of media attention and some nice words of praise from the big four athletics correspondents of the day — Peter Byrne of the *Irish Times*, Jimmy Meagan of the *Irish Press*, Brendan Mooney of the *Cork Examiner*, and of course Tom O'Riordan himself.

On the back of that run, I was listed as joint favourite for the National Junior Cross Country a week later, again in Tullamore. The other favourite was my good friend Padraig Keane, by then running with Clonliffe.

I had good reason to feel confident, and I knew the big carrot for making the top three would be a place on the Irish Junior team for the International Cross Country Championships, as well as a trip to a cross-country race in Spain.

But as life has made a habit of reminding me, things don't always work to plan. I dropped out before a mile was completed, and I can still feel the pain of failure when I think back to that disaster.

It was some years before I got to know Paddy Larkin as a friend and learned of his visionary work in the development of the Harriers' outstanding sports complex.

A man ahead of his time, he brought a dream to fruition, not with State grants or Lottery funding but with the help of loyal clubmates and friends and neighbours. Paddy and his team believed in their town, and the people of Tullamore responded generously. The complex was opened in 1979 and has been a great asset to athletics and to Tullamore.

I was privileged several times to travel with Paddy to major championships abroad. He was wonderful company.

On the day of Paddy's funeral, in October 2006, Harry Gorman arrived at the *Irish Runner* office with a photo from the World Cross Country in Portugal back at the turn of the Millennium. The photo showed Paddy, Sean Callan, Matt Rudden, Harry and myself on a sunny day in Villamoura. We spent may happy days together on that trip and the photograph conjured the memories.

Every year when I covered events at the Tullamore track, Paddy would tap me on the shoulder and present me with a ticket for a slap-up feed in the bar — a generous gesture that meant a lot.

Paddy was a remarkable man, one of a rare breed. He was there to comfort me too that day when nerves and lack of sleep caused me to drop out of the Junior Cross Country, but that was just one of countless acts of kindness.

11

Runner On The Ditch

IT was the Sunday after my great run in the Quinlan Cup and the action returned to Tullamore but shifted to cross-country and the National Junior Championships, for which I had been installed as joint favourite alongside my sometime training pal from Ballyhaunis, Padraig Keane.

My confidence was understandably high, especially since my Quinlan Cup effort had come on the back of several frustrating weeks of injury that had curtailed my training. I took it easy the week following Tullamore and felt I was in shape to give my friend a run for his money.

Padraig was by then running in the colours of Clonliffe and was as strong as a pedigree bull over fields and ditches. But Eddie Hogan and Eddie Spillane, my mentors at Donore, assured me I was ready to win my first national title over the country.

I would ideally have stayed in Dublin the weekend of the race and travelled to Tullamore with the Donore team, but on this occasion I felt honour bound to go home to Ballyhaunis on the Friday and get ready for Saturday's inaugural *Western People* Sports Awards Dinner in Ballina. I had been named Athlete of the Year and knew that it would be a special night out for my parents, who were hugely pleased by the honour.

I had been singled out for an award the previous year, but this was a much bigger deal: a lavish banquet for the award winners across a range of sports, and the legendary Michael O'Hehir presenting the prizes. For good measure, the Mayo Gaelic football icon Gerald Courell was to be inducted to the Hall of Fame, and he and O'Hehir were among my father's heroes. Courell had trained the team that brought the Sam Maguire Cup back to Mayo in 1951, the year I was born.

O'Hehir was a wonderful sports commentator with a unique turn of phrase and boundless enthusiasm. His All-Ireland football and hurling commentaries for Radio Eireann were compulsory listening, as was his annual calling of the Grand National from Aintree for the BBC.

I knew my father would be bitterly disappointed were I to turn down this special opportunity to rub shoulders with those great men. And so I headed west on that weekend more than a little worried that a late Saturday night would produce a hangover in Tullamore on Sunday.

Of course it turned out to be a brilliant night in Ballina and my parents were in terrific form. Michael O'Hehir made a big fuss of me and engaged my dad in a long conversation about football. Dad also got to chat with Gerald Courell and was as excited as if he had 'won the Sweep' — the £50,000 Hospital Sweepstakes pot that was the equivalent of today's Lotto jackpot.

The celebrations rocked on, and by the time our chauffeur, Fr John O'Sullivan of the Augustinian Friary in Ballyhaunis, managed to drag my father from the hotel it was well past midnight.

When we reached Ballyhaunis it was after two, and between exhaustion and the excitement of the evening I struggled to sleep.

It was past five when I managed to doze off and a little after eight when my mother was calling me to remind me Fr O'Sullivan would be picking me up within the hour to drive me to Tullamore.

I felt totally spent and anxious as we set out, and though I slept a little on the journey to Tullamore, I was no better when we arrived. Too tired to even attempt a proper warm-up, I jogged around in something of a daze until it was time to toe the line.

Padraig Keane was quick out of the traps, and though I matched strides with him for almost a mile, my legs felt like two pieces of string.

As Padraig surged ahead my concentration crumbled — and yet I told myself that if I could just keep going I would at least take the silver medal and a place on the Irish team for the upcoming International Cross Country. We were clear of a chasing group that included Eamonn Coghlan, who was a few years younger, and I only needed to hang on for about two more miles to earn myself another big award.

To this day, I find it hard to process the memory of what happened next. All I know is that I came to an abrupt stop, dropped out of the race and watched from the ditch as Padraig coasted to victory.

Of course, it was the lack of sleep and the excitement of the previous night that caused the lapse in concentration. But it was a hard lesson, and I returned to Dublin with the Donore team feeling broken and very confused.

That night I went for a walk across Capel Street Bridge and spent a long hour looking out over the Liffey and trying to come to terms with my deep sense of failure. 'Can you do anything right?' I could again hear my mother's voice.

All these years later, I would still not trade a national junior medal or a foreign trip with an Irish team for the delight I witnessed on my parents' faces that night at the Awards Dinner in Ballina. But on Capel Street Bridge I spent a long time in self-blame mode for the aftermath.

It would be a year before I got the chance to run cross-country for Ireland, and that chance arrived on Clonmel Racecourse, where in wind and rain and mud I finished seventh in the National Senior Cross Country.

Padraig finished sixth that day and we both made the team for the World Cross Country in Cambridge. The demons of Tullamore were at least partly exorcised.

12

Knight Of The Road

IT was only memories that were holding me together as the bus trundled toward Ballyhaunis, through Tuam and Dunmore and on to Cloonfad — towns I had often visited during my running apprenticeship. I thought again of my first ever distance race, on Tuam Racecourse, and how I could easily have quit running that day after the trauma of dropping out.

I recalled the pep talk Mick Nestor gave me after that disaster and how Pat Cribbin insisted he knew there was better in me and there would be good days ahead for me in running if I persevered.

A mile beyond Cloonfad we passed the field where Pat Cribbin collected his first medal for running. He would often regale us with the story of how he had won the half-mile race at a sports in that little field and afterwards cycled the five miles home to Lecarrow, steering the bike with one hand and holding the medal out in front of him all the way home in unabashed admiration.

As with myself, Pat's first sport was boxing and he had good ring form. His uncles, the Moylett brothers, had been champion boxers, and when three of them emigrated to the US they continued to excel in their chosen sport. Now back in Ireland, they were great encouragement to Pat, whose passion for the fight game knew no bounds.

Pat used to hitch the 50-odd miles from Ballyhaunis to Westport in all seasons for sparring practice. To get back, he often hopped onto a carriage of a CIE goods train in Westport station and jumped clear when the train slowed coming through Ballyhaunis station, often well past midnight.

My great pal marched to a different drum.

'I'm Foxy the soup maker,' he'd announce to all and sundry in the playground when we attended national school. He had nicknames for all of his friends and most of the good people of Lecarrow.

Among others there were Cuckoo, an only son, and Horse, noted for his ferocious work ethic. Each sobriquet seemed to perfectly describe the character in question.

It was raining hard in Tennessee when I received the news of Pat's fatal accident. I stumbled across the university campus in a state of shock and disbelief as I read the letter from home, my tears mingling with those pouring from a leaden sky.

And I thought back to the evening I first set foot in the Morton Stadium in Santry. I was into a heavy seam of training at the time, learning all about intervals and speedwork and esoteric concepts like 'fartlek' and 'tempo runs'.

Early that summer I had run a few encouraging track races in established sports, among them Mayo Abbey and Ballyglass. I had taken eagerly to this track racing and was eager to improve my times. Pat kept telling me I had a big future in athletics, and all through that summer he plied me with books about training and racing.

Then he told me about an upcoming three-miler in distant Dublin. The race, organised by BLE, the governing body of athletics, was specifically designed to give aspiring youngsters such as myself a chance to tread the hallowed Santry cinders.

After pleading with my parents, I was given the green light to head for the big city and pursue my innocent dreams. And so I set forth from Ballyhaunis on a bright September morning and linked up with Phillip Morley, who was ferrying a load of cattle to the North Wall.

It was my first time to visit the capital alone and I fretted over how I would find my way from the city centre all the way to Santry. Phillip assured me it would be a doddle, and on the back of a Woodbine packet (the cigarette not the flower) he wrote the number of the relevant bus from O'Connell Street. He also wrote instructions on how to get from Santry back to Heuston rail station.

He dropped me off on Bachelors Walk, beside O'Connell Bridge, and I walked up O'Connell Street absorbed in the teeming colour and hubbub of the city. It would be several hours until I needed to head for Santry, and so I explored my new surroundings while also being careful not to stray too far from O'Connell Street.

On the double-decker bus for Santry that evening, the friendly conductor assured me he would alert me when we reached the stadium. I blurted out to my new friend that I was the best runner for my age in Mayo and was about to break 16 minutes for three miles. I'm still not sure if his smile was one of admiration or pity.

Presently, the old stadium loomed and I found the dressing-room, a converted Nissen hut, where my opponents, a lively bunch, were already togging out in an overpowering fog of wintergreen. I felt anxious and overwhelmed when I eventually started my warm-up, even though the spectators were few and the race was to be purely a time trial.

I thought back to the summer of 1958 when, ear to the radio at home in Ballyhaunis, I had listened to fevered commentary as the great Herb Elliott smashed the world mile record on this very track. The magical figure was still burnt on my brain — 3:54.5. As was the 3:57.5, also inside the previous record, posted by Ireland's own Ronnie Delany in third.

I was then seven and full of innocent wonder, and I loved my father's passion when he told me Delany was the best runner ever to come out of Ireland and had brought great honour to his country.

'Elliott may have broken the world record above in Dublin, but Delany won the race that mattered most: the Olympic final,' was my father's emphatic verdict.

That evening when he sent me to Murrays' shop for cigarettes,

I was still bubbling with excitement. And when he said he would time my run there and back I sprinted away at full tilt.

I can still see Johnny Murray's face as I burst in the door urgently calling for 10 Sweet Afton and hopping on the spot while he took what seemed an eternity to fill the order.

I tired a little on the return journey, 800 yards slightly uphill, but father assured me that if I kept running like that I might one day be a champion — someone people would respect and admire. In the matter of my love of running, he was watering the seed my grandfather Harry Mannion had first sown.

That evening of the three-miler in Santry, I started my warm-up alone but was soon joined by an older athlete, who introduced himself as Mick Hickey from Dundrum, County Tipperary. I believe Mick had sensed my unease and took it upon himself to befriend me, a gesture I have always treasured.

He told me to get stuck in early in the lead group and run as fast as I could for as long as I could. His friendly advice calmed me, and I was further assured when he himself led the field out on the opening lap.

I hung on for dear life in the chasing pack and surprised myself by finishing a highly respectable fifth, having been secretly terrified of trailing home last in my Santry debut.

I was less pleased with my finishing time: 16 minutes and 17 seconds. But my friend Mick assured me it was a good time for a lad of my age. He also offered me further advice about training and racing — again a generous gesture; he was taking the trouble to help and encourage an obvious novice.

After the race I packed my trusty duffel bag and made a quick exit from the stadium; I had an urgent call to make — Pat Cribbin would be waiting patiently by the kiosk on the corner of Knox Street, Ballyhaunis.

And so it was from a public phone box on Santry Road that I broke the news to Pat about my dizzy day in Dublin. He was generous as ever with praise and predicted it was only a matter of time before I would be a regular visitor to the same Santry track.

There were indeed many further races on those famous Santry cinders, including the aforementioned heady evening in 1970 when I ran into the record books over 10,000 metres.

The thoughts of those glory days were swimming around in my mind in September 1976 as the bus got ever closer to home — and as memories flooded back of my brave companion of the road, I wept stinging tears.

13

Breaking The Bonds

And you stand there so calm and deceivingly gay,
And you talk of the weather and the events of the day,
Yet your eyes tell me all that your tongue doesn't say
I'm leaving my Nancy Oh!

THAT song by Eric Bogle was one I long had in my repertoire, singing and music having been twin passions since childhood. On those final miles of my journey home in 1976, the words of that song were on my mind again and the memory of my first day leaving home to work in Dublin came back in vivid focus.

I was deeply upset to be leaving home at 19. I had been well settled in my job as junior postman, but then my two-year term ended, and since there was no vacancy for a senior postman in Ballyhaunis I had a choice: a job as postman in a small town the far end of Mayo or a job in the Central Sorting Office in Dublin's Sheriff Street.

A road race in Sligo helped me decide; it was there I met Eddie Spillane from Donore Harriers, and he proved a key factor in my decision to move to Dublin, which was actually the city of my birth.

I ran well in Sligo, and when I told Eddie I had the option of taking up a job in the capital he assured me that Donore — then a powerhouse of distance running — would welcome me with open arms and look after me well.

Eddie told me I was blessed with rare running talent and added that his namesake at Donore, Eddie Hogan, was the best coach in the land. In short, Hogan was the man who could help me develop my talent to the full.

By now I was training as often as three times a day and was eager for new challenges — even if that meant making the huge sacrifice of leaving home. I had won county and provincial championships on road, track and country and felt I was ready for even greater things.

I was fired up from reading publications such as Padraig Griffin's excellent *Marathon Magazine*, which covered the Irish running scene, and *Athletics Weekly*, which with its coverage of rising superstars like Dave Bedford and Ian Stewart across in England had me dreaming big dreams,

My parents had often told me it was 'only by the Grace of God' I arrived safely into the world in the old Coombe Hospital and eventually got back down to Mayo. I was a premature baby, and my mother — who had already lost a child, my sister, after a home birth — was required to travel to the Coombe for the delivery.

I often thought about how traumatic it must have been for her — making what was probably her first visit to the big city, and then travelling back on the train from Dublin, all alone except for the little bundle she was carrying.

Shortly after my birth, and with survival in doubt, I was given a quick baptism in nearby Francis Street church. But I did survive and made the journey home to Ballyhaunis to join my brother, Tom, in the family unit.

Tom was nine at the time, and when I turned five he was already away boarding in St Jarlath's College, Tuam, about 20 miles from Ballyhaunis. He was the big brother whose attention I craved as a kid but he always seemed to be going away somewhere. By the time I reached 11 he had gone to Dublin to join the Augustinians and study for the priesthood.

Nearing home on that September day in 1976, I remembered again the biannual family outings to visit Tom in the Novitiate at Orlagh, in the foothills of the Dublin mountains. We would travel by train and be picked up at Heuston Station by a friend of the family and ferried out to spend the day with Tom.

They were precious days for me and I remember feeling distraught on every occasion when it came time to leave my brother. There was a bond there that I could not explain and a hurt when leaving him that I could not fathom.

I had that same feeling when it came to leaving home for the first time, and I instinctively knew that both my parents were also experiencing that pit-of-the-stomach turmoil as the time neared for me to head for the railway station and board the train for Dublin.

We tried to make light of it, as we would many another time of leaving. My mother was busying herself in the kitchen and making frequent trips upstairs to check if I had left anything behind in the bedroom.

Just like Nancy in Eric Bogle's song, my mother talked about the weather and the neighbours and other light-touch topics, and my father went for a walk outside, 'to see what the day is going to be like'.

I recalled again the deep anxiety and upset swirling around inside me that morning as I tried — with no great success — to keep the emotions at bay. I was in and out of the house, on the pretext of looking to see if Willie Eagney and his hackney car had arrived to pick me up and ferry me to the station. There was time for another cup of tea and more meaningless talk of the weather to fill the painful silence before Willie pulled up and it was time to leave.

It was then that the dam burst, and there were tears and promises and lingering goodbyes before I ran with my bags to the waiting car and waved a final farewell to the folks.

It was a horrible wrench to be leaving home, a chest-bursting, primal, inner scream that lingered all the way to Dublin and for a long time after I got there too.

14

The Mammy Grimes

EDDIE SPILLANE met me off the train in Dublin and drove me around the city in his little Fiat car. He talked incessantly about running and his beloved Donore Harriers, and the talk helped calm the turmoil I had felt on the train journey from Ballyhaunis. But I was still in turmoil as he checked out the various 'digs' that had been recommended by the Post Office.

There were no vacancies in the first few places we visited. I felt growing relief and was already considering returning home that same evening with a good excuse for not staying in the city. I could always go back to Durkan's Bottling Plant, where I had worked for a few summers while still in college. A couple more 'full up' signs and I would be ready to bolt for home.

But persistence might well have been Eddie Spillane's middle name; eventually he found me digs in the city centre. The sealing of the deal was a daunting experience that still resonates.

We arrived at the blue door on Capel Street to be confronted by an elderly grey-haired man whose name I learned was Mick Grimes. He looked me up and down, and down and up, and listened attentively as Spillane explained how this boarding house had been recommended by the Sorting Office people in Sheriff Street, where I was due to start work the following day.

'I'll have to go in and ask Mammy,' was the astonishing reply to Eddie's thorough and glowing enumeration of my credentials as the perfect lodger. Speculating as to the age and housekeeping capabilities of old Grimes's mother, I was now in a state of high anxiety and bewilderment.

To my great relief, it soon became evident that 'Mammy' was in fact Mick's wife, and a stern woman she proved — she came to the door and gave me such a thorough 'once over' as I would not have expected in a Garda station had I been charged with a serious crime.

When she had satisfied herself as to my pedigree and prospects, Mrs Grimes confirmed she had just one vacancy upstairs; I would be sharing a bedroom with a young man from Sligo who also worked for the Post Office. His name, she said, was Mister Rooney — and I could not figure why she referred to him in such formal terms.

I was becoming unhappier by the minute. This sharing a room with a stranger was not part of the script as I had imagined it. It was traumatic enough to be moving to this unfamiliar and teeming city, but to have to share a room in this house run by these two rather severe and extremely old-fashioned people — I was now ready to do a runner.

I desperately wanted to move on and try one more place, but Eddie gently reminded me that we were running out of options and that Capel Street was only a 20-minute walk from my workplace in Sheriff Street; it was getting late in the day and I should take what was on offer.

With great reluctance I handed over my deposit to the steely Mrs Grimes, who gave me a long list of 'house rules' before telling me 'Daddy' would show me to my room. Of course Daddy turned out to be Mick, the head waiter and general factotum in this eccentric establishment that would be home to me for at least the next six months.

In fact, the Grimeses turned out to be perfectly fair and reasonable landlords, but on that first evening I felt I was about to serve time for some crime I had not committed, and it was with a heavy heart and dragging feet that I said goodbye to Eddie and followed old Mick Grimes up the creaking stairs to my new quarters.

15

Cow Sums And Sallies

PADRAIG ROONEY from Sligo would prove an amiable room-mate on Capel Street but I found my introduction to the Grimes Boarding House a huge challenge. It was my first experience of living away from home and sharing a room with someone I had never met, and I was well out of my comfort zone: homesick, unsettled and more than a little afraid.

As we climbed the stairs, Old Mick Grimes reiterated the numerous house rules and reminded me in very certain terms that if I was late in for Sunday dinner that would be just tough luck — there would be no question of keeping plates in the oven or kettles on the hob for later in the day.

My stomach churned and my head spun as I watched him turn on his heel and shuffle back below. There was no offer of even a cup of tea, and my new room-mate confirmed my misgivings by telling me the best thing about our situation was its relative proximity to the Central Sorting Office.

It was going to be a whole new world for me. Feeling lost, and already missing the warm embrace of a home that was often quite dysfunctional but always felt welcoming and safe, I went for a walk over Capel Street Bridge and for about a mile up along the Liffey quays, trying to calm my swirling emotions.

I dreaded the thought of what might lie ahead the following morning when I was due to report to a Mister Joe Giles, my training officer in Sheriff Street. The only training I was interested in at the time was to do with running, and it now seemed I was about to go back to school, something I had tried from the age of four back in Ballyhaunis but never really taken to.

I was experiencing again the anxiety I suffered every morning during my last few years in primary school. The principal teacher was the terror of our young lives, and I have often wondered since how we ever tolerated, and indeed survived, his wild and brutal ways.

The national school was perched on high ground above the Irishtown road, a short distance outside Ballyhaunis town, and from the yard you could clearly see the crossroads leading to and from Dublin and Galway and other strange and unexplored lands. Every morning we young lads would watch in fear and foreboding as the master's car arrived by the cross at ten to nine.

He would park his car, storm up the steps and herd us into the classroom. As we waited in cold terror for his usual morning tirade, he would sit back in his chair, legs perched on the desk in front of him, and let fly

'Ye smell of laziness!' he would roar. 'I'm going to correct the homework now and I will cut the skin clean down off anyone who has not got his work ready for me to look at!'

We would sit trembling at our desks as he leafed disdainfully through the stack of copybooks we had handed up. He would sort the corrected masterpieces in two piles, the whole while cackling away to himself and from time to time snorting a measure of snuff up his nose.

Then it was time for roll call, and those misfortunates whose homework did not pass muster could look forward to six of the worst across each hand with a sally rod. As he doled out the punishment, his fury rising, the master would often drive himself to exhaustion and literally foam at the mouth.

Later in the morning, when he had somewhat calmed down, he would suddenly spring back into action and announce, 'Round the room for a cow sum!'

That was the order for us to scramble from our desks and, with jotters and pencils in hand, take up positions on our knees all around the room as he barked out the details of some complex equation that involved buying and selling cattle.

When not 'teaching', the master bred prize bulls, and there would be massive relief in the school when it came time for the annual Spring Show in Dublin — an event he always attended and won prizes at too. On the morning when we knew the Spring Show was starting we would cheer loudly as ten to nine came and went with no sign of the dreaded motorcar at the cross. It heralded a week of sweet relief, and it sometimes happened that when he returned triumphant from the Show, our tormentor would be in almost mellow mood and for a few days might even appear human.

But he was totally focused on his 'cow sums' and hardly a day passed but we were assigned this 'on your knees around the room' ritual that always had a bad ending for some.

When he had roared out the details of his cow sum, the master would give us a while to wrestle with the equation. That was a time of white-knuckle terror, and you dared not look to anyone for help or prompting. Then he would bark, 'Around the board!' — and we would gather at the blackboard as he selected one unlucky lad to demonstrate the mathematical process.

If things went downhill for the chosen boy, the master would fly into another rage and storm out of the room, heading for the garden. We would watch from the window as he took his penknife and expertly selected and cut clean a fresh sally rod. Then he would bound back into the classroom and proceed to leather the poor scholar who had fatally miscalculated the price of bulls or heifers or weanlings.

I was lucky enough to escape the worst of the flagellations. What spared me was an ability to memorise and recite poetry, something that greatly pleased the master.

He would have me declaim for the class *The Wayfarer* by Padraig Pearse, Thomas Gray's *Elegy Written in a Country Churchyard* or stanzas from Oliver Goldsmith's *Deserted Village*. And so I was seldom called upon to decipher a cow sum, because the frenzy of whippings was often followed by quiet time that included poetry readings.

For all of us, however, the lash of the willow and the roars of execration would land sooner or later, and in hindsight it is little wonder that I miserably failed Inter Cert maths a few years later.

I felt again that grip of terror and anxiety as I trudged back to Capel Street, wishing I could just turn around and go home. Tomorrow promised to be another anxious day and I doubted very much if sleep would come easily in my strange new abode.

16

The Black And Whites

I STRUGGLED to get even a wink of sleep in my new domicile, a small room with two single beds on the second floor of the digs in Capel Street.

When he realised the depth of my distress, Padraig Rooney, though no older than myself, tried manfully to put me at ease. He recounted how hard he had found his own early days in the big city and the shock to the system when he had first set foot in the Grimes establishment.

The following morning I was up dark and early and went for a short walk across Capel Street Bridge before gulping down a cup of tea and heading out again to find my way to Sheriff Street and my looming appointment with Mr Joe Giles.

Padraig had kindly drawn me a little map of my route, which I diligently followed, and as the city came to life I marvelled at the volume of early-morning motor traffic and the throngs hurrying along the pavements on their way to work. It was a huge change from Ballyhaunis, which seldom woke from sleep before 10am.

The Central Sorting Office in Sheriff Street was a massive structure and a place to which I took an instant dislike. I got there well ahead of the appointed time and waited nervously for my instructor to arrive.

Joe Giles was a dapper little man with no time for the small talk that might have eased my jangling nerves. He told me he would be training me in all aspects of letter sorting and that within a few weeks I should be capable of delivering the post across several city routes.

Again I experienced panic mode, and again I had flashbacks to those 'cow sum' ordeals in National School. Bizarrely, I was almost waiting for Mr Giles to outline the punishments that awaited failure in any of the tasks he was about to assign me.

I was soon installed at a bench facing an array of pigeon holes — small boxes labelled with placenames. A large clock hung a few feet above my head. I was about to be shown the finer points of 'primary sorting', and for the next several weeks this and the 'facing table' would be what I called with bitter irony 'my stamping ground'.

Presently a small man with one leg shorter than the other arrived with a barrow of letters and landed hundreds of them in front of me. Sorting them was a slow process at first, and every few minutes Joe Giles would arrive back to see how I was progressing.

I beavered away, and after what felt like an hour of industrious endeavour I looked up at the clock and discovered to my dismay that only 15 minutes had elapsed. For the next few weeks that same clock would be the bane of my life as time hung heavy and slow and the sorting experience became a dreary daily drudgery.

I would work my way through the pile, trying manfully not to keep glancing overhead at the clock, which always seemed to be recording the time at well less than half speed. Then, just when I was beginning to feel good about the progress made, and with only a handful left to sort, the small man would appear around the corner pushing his barrow. It was uncanny how he always arrived on cue — just as I looked forward to a short break.

There was only one escape from the sorting bay and that was assignment to the 'facing table', where you stood for hours with several other bored souls 'facing' letters — turning them address side up — for the sorting process. I dreaded that facing table and did my best to avoid being assigned there, because if time stood still in the sorting department it went into reverse at the facing table.

Working in a confined space was an alien experience that I found hard to handle. Time dragged interminably and the overhead clock mocked my misery. I missed the freedom of movement I had enjoyed during my years as a junior postman, freewheeling with the wind in my spokes, happy and contented on the open roads. Now I might as well have been in Mountjoy Jail, and to make matters worse I was still brutally homesick.

That facing table was universally dreaded, but Joe Giles assured me it was an indispensable step on my way to becoming a fully fledged postman.

What kept me going during that first month in Sheriff Street were my evening visits to the Donore Harriers clubhouse in Islandbridge. Eddie Spillane or John Phelan would pick me up at Capel Street and drive me to Hospital Lane, and it was there that I met some of my heroes who were already legends of distance running — the likes of Tom O'Riordan, Jim McNamara, Mick Connolly, Tommy Redican, Willie Dunne.

I remember my first evening in that tiny clubhouse. Tom O'Riordan, togged out in the famous Black and White, was deep in conversation with Jim McNamara, talking of a race he had recently run in Spain.

I had seen Tom from a distance a few times and was present the day he and Danny McDaid arrived as special guests to race over three miles at the Athenry Sports. That day, inspired no doubt by the presence of the two superstars, my pal Padraig Keane and I fought a torrid battle in the supporting 'open three mile' race, which Padraig won narrowly. Padraig and I were too awestruck to approach our heroes, but we later thumbed our way back home with soaring spirits.

That evening when I first shared a dressing-room with Tom O'Riordan and his hardy comrades always remained special. Tom was king of cross-country at the time, an Olympian and one of the sweetest movers ever to grace a track. He was a little aloof, but in a shy and not an arrogant way. It was a few years before

I discovered he was a most engaging conversationalist and we became firm friends.

On Tuesday nights as we Harriers wended our way out of Hospital Lane, Tom and Jim Mac would set a scorching pace up the steep Knockmaroon Hill and far beyond. The Donore sessions were the stuff of legend, and when I was part of those sessions I felt I had reached the promised land.

Then came a day in Clonmel when I made the Donore scoring team that won the National Interclubs Cross Country Championships and cried tears of delight at being part of O'Riordan's Black and White brigade. It made up for all the days of drudgery in the Central Sorting Office, and by then I had escaped and was happily delivering the post in Swords and greater Fingal.

And when O'Riordan wrote about the race in the *Irish Independent* of the following Monday and confirmed I had made the Irish senior team for the upcoming International Cross Country in Cambridge, England, I felt several feet taller than my five-foot-seven.

By then I had also left Capel Street and was comfortably settled in a flat in Philipsburg Avenue, Fairview.

I bought not one copy of the *Independent* but the entire stack in the nearest newsagents and read and reread Tom's race report. I even read aloud the part about these two young West of Ireland men, Keane and Greally, and their breakthrough to the senior international ranks.

Padraig and I had come a long way since that first cross-country race in Hollymount. We had both taken the train to Dublin and Padraig was now with Clonliffe Harriers. It seemed life could hardly get better.

17

Against The Grain

EDDIE HOGAN was my first coach. A quiet man with a huge reputation, he played a key role in the success I achieved in the colours of Donore Harriers.

Eddie was the man in charge at the cramped Donore clubhouse at the end of Hospital Lane, Islandbridge. He was an extremely patient man but there were many times that in my youthful exuberance I severely tested his equanimity as he tried to tie me into a sensible training regime.

Back in those early days in Donore, I went full tilt at everything and especially loved having a go at the best seniors in the club.

Poor Eddie continued to preach the gospel of planning, restraint and incremental improvement. He tried his best to bring discipline and regularity to my training, but I'm afraid that for all his legendary genius and people skills he was bound to fail.

Eventually, when I had been some months at the club and had achieved much early success despite the extreme unorthodoxy of my approach to training — the 10-mile runs after midnight were only half of it — Eddie wrote me a letter I wish I had kept.

In that letter he carefully explained his theory on training, theory that when put into practice had built Donore into a distance superpower. He also took pains to remind me that talent was not enough — structure and discipline were paramount to achieving success in sport and life.

Alas, Eddie might as well have tried to catch the wind as to try harnessing me to anything like a regular routine. He was as understanding as a man could be, and when many years after those heady days in Donore we became close friends, he never once reminded me how I had pushed him to the limits.

I often wonder how things would have turned out had I stayed in Ireland under Eddie's tutelage. Not only was he the most knowledgeable coach I ever met, I believe he understood me and instinctively knew, despite my self-will and indiscipline, how to get the best out of me.

It seems that from early childhood I was always pulling at the leash and pushing the limits.

I was only six when I flagged down the Oatfield Sweets van, hitched a ride to Monica Hunter's sweet shop, about a mile from our house, and arrived back home to find my mother and several neighbours in panic as they scoured lanes and fields for the truant child.

I was seven when I inherited my brother's blue-and-white bike and became the terror of the neighbourhood, flying recklessly in all directions.

Around that time there was the day I went wandering off through the fields, across a river and into the bog. I had seen from my bedroom window the jib of a dredger on the bog and my curiosity was piqued. I would hardly be writing these lines today had the operator of that dredger not been alert.

He would later tell of how he was amused and astonished to see a small boy advancing toward him across the wide, brown expanse. He looked away for a few seconds — and when he looked again the waif was nowhere to be seen.

What happened was that I had come across a boghole filled with water and was curious as to how deep it might be. I put a foot in the water, and when the other foot slipped I went feet first into a morass that sucked me in and pulled me down. I was in blind panic, my head was scarcely above water, and I was being pulled under.

The dredger operator acted on impulse, jumping from his machine and running to where he had lasted sighted me. When he arrived I was submerged but for my head, and it took all that man's considerable strength to pull me from what would have been a muddy grave.

Once rescued, I broke free and, sobbing hysterically, ran for home. I recall vividly my mother's reaction when I burst through the door drenched to the skin and bawling with fright. She took one look at me and in her own panic beat me around the room, adding greatly to my distress.

It was only when she calmed down and took stock of the crisis that she started to hug me and talk soothing words — but I never forgot her panicked reaction to the slime-caked apparition that came through the front door that day.

Several years later I had another close call involving water, this time when I almost drowned on Boone Lake in East Tennessee. That day I was out on a barge in a secluded cove in the company of two lovely Tennessee ladies. I will return to that episode presently.

18

From Pillar To Post

MY first day alone on the postal beat ended in disaster. Ill-prepared, I failed to properly sort my load, eventually lost my bearings and struggled exhausted back to base in late afternoon with most of it undelivered — and, not for the first time, a mother's disapproving voice echoed in my head: 'Can you do nothing right?'

I had endured several weeks in the huge sorting office, where time passed slowly and the daily routine numbed the brain.

My supervisors must have sensed my discomfort at working indoors, because eventually one of them suggested I be tried out on a postal route, something that was music to my ears — anything would be better than the sense of enslavement I felt while sorting and 'facing', and the prospect of being able to walk about while delivering letters was hugely appealing.

I was assigned for training to a young postman on a route close to the central sorting office: an area encompassing Lower Sherriff Street, Oriel Street and a number of flat complexes.

I traversed this route for a week with my mentor but found he had not the slightest interest in showing me the ropes. From the moment we left the sorting office each morning, I heard only four words from him: 'We have to fly.' This lad set himself a tight target for his work and demanded to be finished and back home in record time. He had no room for small talk; his urgency and body language told me one thing: 'Follow me if you can, but I'm not here to tell you much.'

And so when at the end of a week my postman 'mentor' went on holidays, I was given charge of his beat. My anxiety levels were in orbit that Monday morning as I turned up at Sherriff Street for a 6.30 start. I had picked up little or nothing while blindly following the fastest postman in the east of Dublin city. He had not allowed me do any preparatory sorting of letters — that would have slowed him down and delayed his return home for second breakfast.

It took me ages to sort the letters for the route on that Monday morning, and I was at least an hour behind all the other postmen when I finally headed out on what I hoped was the route we had covered the previous week.

I was okay for the first half-hour and felt I was making progress. Then the whole thing unravelled; I lost my bearings and started to panic.

I entered a flat complex and was immediately surrounded by housewives impatiently enquiring, all at the same time, if I had post for them.

'Have you a letter for number 15, Mister?' one enquired, while simultaneously the others threw in their competing demands — number 24, 42, 53, and so on. I was being ambushed but I did my best to check through my bundles, dreading all the time I might be giving out letters to the wrong people.

I soon bolted from that flats complex without finishing my delivery and tried to find some of the other streets and addresses on the route. It was all highly distressing, and my growing panic and frustration were no help.

It was well after midday that I arrived back to the sorting office having conceded defeat and with only a third of the round completed. My supervisor turned out to be a kindly and understanding man and on seeing my distress quietly took the mailbag from me and assured me I was not the first postman to mess up on his first day out.

I was beyond consolation but hugely relieved when my supervisor suggested I go back indoors for another few days and leave the delivering to a more experienced hand.

I felt a total failure that day and was sorely tempted to get the train back to Ballyhaunis the very same afternoon. I decided in the end that bad as the situation was I could not face the shame of arriving home and telling my parents I had quit the job. I had disappointed them enough in my short life, and I resolved to stay in Sherriff Street for at least another month and see how things worked out.

Within a few weeks, I had an answer to my many prayers when Eamonn Ryan, an executive in Sherriff Street and also a running friend, suggested a postal route becoming vacant in Swords might be just the job for me. It would be out in the open air — delivering to a few housing estates as well as cycling well out into the countryside. There would also be a financial bonus in the form of an allowance for travelling to Swords, a trip I would make in the van delivering bags from Sherriff Street to the Swords sub-post office.

Eamonn was a member of Civil Service Harriers and knew that my running career was just taking off. Having heard about my disastrous unfinished round and also noted my discomfort in the sorting office, he was eager to help. His suggestion that I give Swords a whirl proved a godsend, and I felt my prayers — and no doubt my mother's — must have been heard on high.

And so one bright summer morning I hitched a lift on the mail van out of Sherriff Street and headed for my new job in Swords, where I struck up an instant friendship with the first man I met there, a postman by the name of Harry, who at 6.30am, sitting on the steps of the sub-post office, offered me a large bottle of Guinness to celebrate my new position — an offer I was quick to decline.

19

Fangs For The Memory

I WAS soon happy as a lark in my new job as a postman in Swords, and this time around I found an instructor — a young man named Michael — who was considerate and conscientious in showing me the round I would take over.

Swords was then more a country village than the bustling satellite town it is today, but already there were a number of housing estates springing up. I was assigned to Rathbeale Estate and Glasmore Park, which between them had about 600 houses — a lovely, handy detail when it came time to deliver monthly ESB or other bills, one for every house.

It did take a while to get to grips with the very odd numbering system in Rathbeale; some quirk of the planning department had decreed you could have number 220, quickly followed by something like 319, all highly confusing at first for this rookie postman.

I developed my own unique method of delivering to the estates. I would park my bike and literally run through the round, leaping over gates and walls, well shod too in heavy army boots, all calculated to turn the morning shift into something of a training session.

Before starting deliveries to the two housing estates, I would cycle up Pinnock Hill, in the direction of Dublin City, and deliver to the houses en route, as well as those in Rathingle, a bit farther away.

I would follow up my housing estate deliveries by cycling out into the country, with Radio Luxembourg blaring away on a transistor radio I had strapped to the basket of my bike.

I often held that same transistor radio to my ear on midnight training runs out around Fairview, Sutton and the Hill of Howth. Everything I did then seemed what might nowadays be described as 'left field', and I could never really figure out why that was so.

I was fortunate in Swords to meet up with another array of characters — a handful of postmen all with their own unique and endearing traits.

Harry, whom I had met on the post office steps that first morning, became a staunch ally, even though I had spurned his offer of an early-morning drink.

I smile when I think of that first-morning introduction as we waited for the postmistress to open the premises. When I declined the offer of stout, Harry, as casual as you like, reached into an inside pocket and produced a small bottle of whiskey, better known as a baby Power.

'Have a little sip of this to get you started,' he urged. But again I declined.

Though only in his early 40s, Harry had already fallen too much in love with alcohol, and it led to his death before he reached 50. I somehow felt I understood the need that stalked my friend — even back then I had begun to use drink as a crutch to help me through bouts of depression.

I recall a night when I had been about a month in Dublin, looking out the window of my bedroom in Capel Street and feeling totally submerged in a pit of loneliness and depression. It was a Thursday night and most of the lodgers had gone across to Grainger's Pub in Great Strand Street. I had never felt so alone, and on pure impulse I went to the pub for a few bottles of Guinness that I ended up drinking out of a cup in my room.

The alcohol tasted good and it reminded me of Sundays as a kid when, proud as punch, I would sit on the high stool beside my father in Peter Hannon's pub in Ballyhaunis, sipping out of that small glass that my father called a pony of stout. It would be many years down the line that I would come to realise that, like my friend Harry, I too had, almost without noticing, become dependent on alcohol.

I soon discovered that Thursday nights in Grainger's Pub could be good fun in the company of fellow lodgers from Grimes's Boarding House. I enjoyed my few pints back then, the company and the crack, but by the middle of the 1970s alcohol was already beginning to work its cunning, baffling and powerful spell on me in a very unhealthy way.

Back on the postal beat in Swords, I also greatly enjoyed meeting Billy, a wizened little man who drove his own Honda 50 on deliveries. Billy was quite contrary and for some reason hated more than anything for people to ask him questions.

I have one abiding memory of Billy — and a day he was detailed to collect the cash from the telephone coin box on Swords Main Street. He was in the cramped kiosk, engrossed in his task, when the door was pulled open and he received a firm tap on the shoulder.

'Excuse me,' said the very tall and rather brusque stranger — just as Billy had opened the coin box and was easing out the tray. Startled by the sudden invasion of his space, Billy dropped the tray and with it a veritable jackpot of copper and nickel that went spinning onto the pavement and along the gutter.

'I'm so sorry,' said the stranger. 'I was just across the road when I spotted you and thought you'd be just the man to direct me to the road for Skerries. Let me help you pick up the coins, my dear fellow.'

Straightening to his full height of five-foot-five, Billy took the tall intruder by the lapels and backed him out of the box before launching into his answer to the question of the road to Skerries.

'Excuse me! Did you really risk your life and cross the busy main street to ask me the road to Skerries because you thought I was just the man? Well sir, I have news for you. I'm not just the man, your man or any man's. I'm my own man — a postman and not a bloody tourist information officer.

'Now I can only suggest that you risk your life again and cross the street and continue on up until you get to the Garda Station. Maybe you will find just the man in there — if they don't arrest you first.'

Billy was a fiery one indeed, and we wound him up without mercy but always with good humour.

I have many warm memories of those carefree days delivering the post in Swords, and one other incident that continues to bring a smile concerns the little terrier that sank fangs deep into my thigh out in Brackenstown, at one of the last houses on my country run.

For several weeks I had been teasing the same terrier every time I walked up the short drive to his house. As soon as I approached the gate, the terrier would spring from his kennel and charge at me, barking and snarling savagely.

I got a serious fright the first time he attacked, before noting to my great relief that the chain attached to his collar pulled him up short just before he reached the gravel walk leading to the house. And so I made a little mark in the ground — inches from the point at which I knew he would be stopped short.

That formula worked a dream for a number of weeks, and I must admit I took a certain delight in teasing the poor animal. Then one day as I brazenly picked out my safe spot, he came flying — but this time, to my shock and horror, he made a direct hit on my right thigh and sank those razor-sharp teeth deep into flesh.

I screamed and swore in agony, but he hung on, biting and snarling, for what seemed an eternity, before eventually cutting loose and retreating to his kennel. He had exacted revenge in spades.

It was then that I saw a curtain move in an upstairs window, and I figured that the occupant, fed up with watching me tease his beloved pet, had planned the assault by adding a few judicious links to the chain.

I knocked on the door, hoping to get first aid for the mangled leg, but no answer was the stern reply. And so with the limb already stiffening, I jumped on my bike and rode as fast as I could back to Swords, where the tetanus jab and other injections administered by Dr Greenan were almost as frightening and agonising as the dog bite.

There followed a few painful days on the bike, after which I was always mindful of giving my feisty little nemesis a wide berth; he had earned my respect.

That Christmas brought a pleasant surprise when the dog's owner opened the door and handed me a card with a generous tip inside.

'You're a sound man,' he said. 'But you were being a little bollox to my dog and I had to teach you a lesson. I was often going to report you to the postmistress, but I think you have learned your lesson.

'I'm sorry now about what happened, but I have to admit I thought it very funny to see Prince swinging out of your leg that day. Go on now, enjoy the Christmas and stay well clear of barking dogs!'

I shook the man's hand and laughed with him and admitted he had indeed taught me a valuable lesson — one I would never forget.

20

Run On The Wild Side

FAMILY matters weighed heavy on my mind that September morning in 1976 as the bus trundled on toward Ballyhaunis. I needed light relief, and as we rolled through the townlands of Gurrane and Johnstown fond memories came flooding back.

There was the home of Nora Ruane in Johnstown. I smiled as I recalled a wild November morning some years earlier and Nora on her trusty bicycle, pressing hard into the gale, heading for early Mass in Ballyhaunis. Our neighbour was a daily communicant and mother of two priests, and it was said affectionately in our house that there was no difficulty or disaster, natural or otherwise, could keep Nora from her religious duties.

On that wild winter's morning of yore I had marvelled at Nora's faith and devotion, but my own faith at the time was focused more on one Emil Zatopek, the multiple Olympic champion famed for his Spartan training in heavy army boots and in all weathers as well as his passionate, tortured running style.

It was Pat Cribbin who introduced me to articles and books about the legendary 'Czech Locomotive' — and with the innocent enthusiasm of youth I was determined to copy the training of the master.

That morning when I looked out the bedroom window I was delighted to see the rain sweeping across John Hunt's Hill beyond. Like Nora, I revelled in the wind and rain but for different reasons; for me it was because Zatopek had insisted that the wilder elements made you a tougher, better athlete.

And so when, shortly after dawn, I met Nora Ruane on her way to Mass, I was bounding along at a fair speed with the monsoon gale to my back, in hobnail boots, corduroy trousers and oilskin jackets. I had about eight miles to complete and I was a young man in a hurry.

I gave my neighbour a wide berth, extending to her the full courtesy of the road as she battled into the teeth of the storm. But I had continued only a few yards on my merry gallop when I heard her calling after me.

I stopped in my tracks and looked back, and sure enough, Nora had dismounted her machine and was beckoning with urgent words and gestures. Of course I ran back to what I guessed must be a neighbour in distress, only to be met by the breathless question:

'Francis, Francis! Is there something wrong at home that has you out running somewhere at this hour?'

I assured my mother's friend that all was well in the Greally homestead, my mother and father being sound asleep in their bed and for good measure in the whole of their health. I added that my own apparently eccentric behaviour was nothing but the pursuit of athletic excellence as recommended by the famous Olympian Emil Zatopek.

Bemused but obviously relieved, Nora continued on her way, as did I on mine.

An hour later when I arrived back home drenched to the skin, Nora was sitting by the hearth drinking tea with my mother. I passed no remark and went upstairs to wash and get ready for work.

Presently Nora left, and my mother revealed the reason for the surprise visit. The good woman had been shocked and worried: she was quite certain, she told my mother, that if I persisted with these crazy pre-dawn excursions I would end up with pleurisy, pneumonia or a strained heart — or a combination of all three.

Of course I reassured my poor mother to the contrary and offered in evidence copious Zatopek quotes on training and good health. To further calm her fears I insisted she read an article about the great man in *World Sports* magazine. And in the following weeks and months whenever I met Nora along the road, I made sure to demonstrate my continuing vitality by giving her a broad smile and a cheery wave.

The bus was into the home straight now and passing the boreen leading into the village of Lecarrow, the start of the Round the Road circuit where my distance running career had begun. From there to the house in Devlis was just a quarter of a mile, a stretch of road I had often used for interval training.

It was the final stretch of my long journey home and the whirlwind of mixed emotions and anxiety had not abated. I had told my parents the month of my arrival home, but not the day, and I hoped the element of surprise might be enough to keep at bay — at least for a few days — any searching questions they might have about my last, troubled year in the hills of East Tennessee.

21

Following The Dream

THE bus rounded the final bend toward Devlis and there was the old house, the hearth and home I had left four years earlier to chase dreams of running glory. My thoughts went back to the very evening I had made the final decision to accept the scholarship offer from East Tennessee State University.

I was all of 21— ancient by US freshman criteria — but I wanted to grasp the opportunity to travel Stateside when Neil Cusack and Eddie Leddy recruited me for the cross-country team known as the Irish Brigade. And so I abandoned a secure position — permanent and pensionable, as my father reminded me — delivering the post out of Swords.

He also reminded me that I would be first in line to get my own round in Ballyhaunis when the incumbent retired within a few years. I knew it was his dearest wish for me that I inherit the town job, but I was far from keen on the idea.

It was on a visit home to Devlis, on one of those dank, grey days when the cold rain would sweep across John Hunt's Hill, opposite the old homestead, that after much pondering I finally took the momentous decision to travel. There was no master plan, just the impulse to get moving in a new direction.

Back in March of that year, at the International Cross Country Championships in Cambridge, Neil had a long chat with me and told me all about the running programme at East Tennessee State.

It seemed to be working well for him and Eddie Leddy; both made the Irish team for the Munich Olympics that year, Neil in the 10,000 metres and Eddie in the steeplechase. Neil assured me that with the right support and coaching there was no reason I could not make it to the 1976 Olympics in Montreal, four years hence.

It seemed Coach Dave Walker in ETSU had been monitoring my progress ever since I broke the Irish junior 10,000m record two years previously, and when I made the team for Cambridge he gave Cusack and Leddy the green light to recruit me. When I learned he was also offering a scholarship to my good friend Ray McBride, I felt I was making the right decision.

There were other decisive factors. A couple of months after our Cambridge conversation, I watched Cusack and Leddy, then in full pre-Olympic mode, stride out on a training run near my modest lodgings on the North Strand. They seemed a different breed, almost superhuman as they floated effortlessly over the ground. The sight of them moving sweetly in unison that day made a deep impression; they represented a marvellous new world. The scholarship to ETSU meant I too could soon be heading for the promised land.

The one nagging doubt I had about going was the fact I would be leaving my parents isolated. By now my father had retired from his job at the Augustinian Friary and his bouts of depression had worsened. My mother had also experienced depression, following the death of her sister Eileen, but had rallied well and was always there to support my father. But he went into rapid decline as soon as he stopped working, and I resolved then to never give up working while I still had my faculties.

I often felt that if I stayed at home for very long I too might become clinically depressed. Ever since my late teens I had experienced what I would many years later recognise as bouts of depression, feelings of greyness that might last several days. It was like a filter or a shade that dampened the spirit, and I was reluctant to discuss the affliction with anyone for fear they would suggest I had inherited my parents' problems.

I had experienced some dark days and nights in Dublin too. During one such slump I stayed in my flat in Philipsburg Avenue on the night of my 21st birthday, while in a nearby pub friends celebrated my coming of age. That should have been a warning sign for me to address the problem — but then I was never great at heeding warning signs.

I slept the night on my decision to head Stateside. The following day I stood in the doorway of our house and watched the rain lashing the hedgerows and dripping off the wires, and felt again the deep need to escape — for a while at least.

I turned around and looked at my father and mother sitting at the hearth. They were both in reasonable physical health. My mother in particular was energetic and seemed willing and able to look after my father for at least the next four years. They had managed okay since I moved to Dublin, and though I knew the leaving would mean heartbreak, I also knew that if I did not seize this opportunity I might live to regret it.

'What do you think I should do about Tennessee?' I asked my mother.

'I think you've already made up your mind,' she replied. 'I think it's an opportunity you cannot let pass by. Don't be worrying about us — go and see the world and make the best of what they're offering you in Tennessee.'

My father stayed silent but I knew my mother was speaking for both of them.

And so I would head for the hills of East Tennessee, and I convinced myself it was my destiny to go there. I had long harboured ambitions to become a journalist, like my good friend Tom O'Riordan, who had also gone the US Collegiate route and was now writing for the *Irish Independent*. As a clincher, Neil Cusack had assured me there was a great Journalism and English Literature programme at ETSU.

'I'll go, but if I don't like it there or if either of you need me I will be back in a flash,' I told my parents.

'May God direct you to do the right thing and I think you're making the right decision,' my mother said.

'I think it's time for a cup of tea,' I said.

I put on the kettle and looking across the kitchen saw tears well up in my father's eyes. Both my parents had relied on me to coax him out of his darker moods. I had found ways of doing that, oftentimes just winding him up as a way to drag him out of himself. I brought my own kind of fun and laughter into our house, and I knew that all three of us were going to sorely miss that over the next few years.

I never felt closer to my parents than on the night before I set out for Tennessee. A couple of neighbours — Rita Webb and Willie Coyne — had combined to organise a farewell party and a whip-round for me in the Parochial Hall in Ballyhaunis, a gesture I have always remembered with great fondness.

All my friends were there to wish me well. It was a special night for my parents to see their son receive this type of local recognition and I knew they were deeply grateful to Rita and Willie.

As we walked home from that reception there was very little talk, and not a word was said about the leaving that had to be faced by the three of us the following day. Each of us in our own way dreaded the parting that would come in the morning.

22

Missing In Manhattan

I MET Ray McBride and his parents, Bob and Kathleen, at Shannon as the pair of us were setting off on our great adventure to Tennessee. Ray's sister Margaret and his younger brother Shane were there too that day.

I had hooked up with Ray after winning the New Year's Eve Round the Houses race in Galway in the late 1960s. We became fast friends in every sense, and the McBride house in the Claddagh had since become very much a second home for me.

As we bade our farewells at Shannon, Kathleen shook my hand and made me solemnly promise to look after Ray on the journey. I had turned 21 and Ray was a couple of years younger, and so it was natural she assumed I was slightly the more responsible. If she had guessed what would happen to Ray in New York, I doubt she would have let him board the plane.

The first leg of our journey took us to New York, where we discovered a stunning world of skyscrapers, subways and teeming sidewalks, and for a few days from our base in the Belmont Plaza Hotel we spent many happy hours — eyes full of wonder — exploring the vast city.

The night before leaving New York for Tennessee, we visited my Aunt Dell in the Bronx. My father's sister, Dell had emigrated in her early twenties, married and raised a son and daughter on her own after her husband, Pat Hughes, died suddenly.

She lavished us with hospitality and some welcome dollars too and, as we left, insisted I phone her when we got back to the Belmont Plaza, she being concerned for our safety in the concrete jungle.

Of course I was happy to make the call, and with the hotel in sight, I found a phone booth on a street corner in downtown Manhattan. Ray waited on the pavement — or so I thought.

When I had reassured Aunt Dell we were back safely at base and all was right with the world, I stepped out of the phone box to find my pal had vanished into the night.

I wasn't alarmed; I returned to our room in the Belmont fully expecting the Galway joker to leap, laughing hysterically, from a wardrobe. But no — the room was silent and there was no trace of Ray anywhere in the hotel.

An hour passed and there was still no sign of him. I was getting worried and in some trepidation ventured back out to search the city streets and bars and diners, which search proved fruitless.

Back in the hotel I phoned Neil Cusack and Kevin Breen, also Tennessee bound and staying with friends elsewhere in the Big Apple. I was now more than a little panicked; Ray was the youngest of our group, and as I recalled his mother's earnest words to me in Shannon I felt hugely responsible for his welfare.

'Give him a bit of time and I'm sure he'll get back okay,' Neil advised.

I dared not call Aunt Dell — I didn't want to upset her — and so I paced the room, my stomach a knot of anxiety and all kinds of wild imaginings in my head.

Several hours passed, and I was on the point of phoning the police when the door burst open and Ray was framed in the entrance, an apparition palpably stressed but otherwise unharmed. What wonderful relief!

My first impulse was to punch him, but I stifled the urge and roared at him instead. When he had calmed me down he relayed a story I still cherish for its innocence.

While I was phoning Aunt Dell, a convoy of fire engines sped past with sirens wailing. A part-time firefighter back home in Galway — the station was across the road from his house — Ray was seized by curiosity and set off in very hot pursuit of the engines. He ran several blocks, but for all his great speed and endurance the engines got away.

When he gave up the chase, he realised he had lost his bearings. Worse still, in the days since our arrival he had neglected to remember the name of our hotel, much less the address. And so for hours he walked and ran hither and thither, alone and bewildered in deepest Manhattan.

At last, in a flash of inspiration he waved down a yellow cab. He was unable to give the cabbie a destination, so they toured the city looking for a familiar street-mark that might jog Ray's memory. Just when all seemed hopeless and as the meter kept revolving, the word 'plaza' flashed on Ray's befuddled brain.

'Take me to the Plaza!' he blurted.

Soon they drew up outside the palatial edifice of the same name near Central Park, where Ray had to sheepishly admit that the 'plaza' he had in mind was slightly smaller.

'Dammit, kid!' roared the frustrated cabbie. 'After all this driving around you'd imagine something would ring a darned bell!'

'That's it!' said Ray as another light came on. 'The bell! We're staying at the Belmont Plaza!'

It was the first of many hair-raising adventures for McBride and myself over the following four years.

23

Heartbreak Hills

AS the bus slowed on the way into Devlis I had the sudden, terrifying intuition that my whole life was unravelling. I was nursing bitter regret over the way the past four years had turned out, and the bounce gained from sharing stories and drinking pints with Neil Cusack back in Limerick had completely evaporated.

I wondered if things might have turned out differently had I stayed delivering the letters around Swords and continued training and progressing steadily under Eddie Hogan at Donore.

Eddie had coached me to achieving a national 10,000-metre record and a place on the Irish cross-country team. He had seemed to understand me and been willing to work with me however hard I tested his patience. It was a futile exercise now to be looking back and wishing for what might have been, because in the end game I knew deep down that I alone was responsible for the choices I had made during my time in Tennessee.

I thought ruefully of a song by the country legend George Jones: *'I've had choices since the day that I was born/ There were voices that told me right from wrong/ If I had listened I wouldn't be here today/ Living and dying with the choices I made.'*

I remembered the September day I first arrived on the ETSU campus. The wonder of it all when Ray McBride and I touched down at Tri-Cities Airport. How full of hope and enthusiasm I had been!

We were met that day at the airport by Coach Dave Walker — a big man, a former professional gridiron footballer — who drove us back to Johnson City, the place that would be home to us both for the next four years.

He took us straight to the university and, with Neil Cusack, Eddie Leddy, PJ Leddy and Kevin Breen, we sat in circle on the floor of his office and listened to him outline plans for the collegiate cross-country season.

It was going to be a tough season and Coach Walker informed us he would be relying on his newest recruits to run well for the team known as the Irish Brigade, all the members being from the Old Country and proud of it.

With Neil and Eddie just back from the Munich Olympics and PJ Leddy and Kevin both running well, Coach Walker had high hopes for the National Collegiate Championships in Houston, Texas.

I remembered his words to Ray and myself that day: 'The reason you have arrived here is because I know you have talent — but I want you both to know from the very start that talent is not enough unless you have a corresponding work ethic. The one thing I will ask you both, as I ask all my runners, is that you give it your best shot.'

Then he dropped a bombshell. He explained that although Ray and myself had been promised full scholarships that would include rooms, meals, books and tuition, providing us with meals was going to be a 'small problem' because the Conference in which we would compete forbade scholarship athletes to avail of free meals.

He had, however, 'a solution to the problem' — he had jobs lined up in the women's cafeteria, where we would wash dishes for a couple of hours each day, earning a little pocket money and getting fed into the bargain.

It was not exactly as we had dreamed when signing on the dotted line, but we took it all in our stride and decided any chance to make a few dollars should be seized with both hands.

That dish-room experience in the women's cafeteria turned out to be a fun time for Ray and me. Every day we got to meet lines of lovely, friendly female students as they handed us their lunch trays and dishes for sorting and stacking in the giant washer. There was time for chat — and of course, as they repeatedly told us, they just adored our Irish accents and our 'gift of the gab'. We were more than happy to let them hear us talk.

We came to know Coach Walker. And we got to know him even better when his blue Buick cruised into the parking lot outside our dormitory at 6.30 every weekday morning that autumn, or fall — the signal it was time for our six-mile run around the roads skirting the campus.

Just back from Munich, Neil and Eddie were both on fire from the experience of competing in their first Olympiad and they led us out on those morning runs, which in fairness were not so fast as to be difficult.

Then after morning classes and our two-hour stint in the dish-room, we would head for the mountains, where Coach Walker would meticulously log our splits over 11 lung-bursting miles, before returning to campus for a track session.

For McBride and myself this was our baptism of fire and it took time to adjust. And all the time we were aware of Coach Walker trackside, timing our efforts with great precision. The session over, he would gather us together to dispense words of encouragement or instruction.

Years later, Walker admitted to me it was actually Cusack who set most of the training sessions at ETSU, something I had quietly suspected all along.

Having arrived at ETSU a lot less fit than I needed to be, I was on the back foot from day one of those sessions.

In those days, it was a requirement that scholarship students undergo a full medical, including chest X-ray, at the US Embassy. By all accounts this was a thorough going over, and if you failed in any aspect you would not be travelling Stateside.

I had been warned during the summer about this medical and someone had suggested I might fail because of a prominent and somewhat unsightly vein on my right leg. And so my GP suggested I have the vein tied off and arranged for the operation in the Mater.

The surgery went to plan, but it was by then mid-August and I was headed for Tennessee in September. It took me almost the full month to recover from the operation and get back running — but for fear he would cancel my scholarship I chose to hide all this from Coach Walker.

And so I struggled badly on those mountain runs and the bright fall sunshine did little to cheer me as I chased Cusack and Leddy up the hills and at every checkpoint was reminded by Coach Walker: 'You're letting them get away from you! You need to close that gap!'

I had been well used to savage sessions with Donore Harriers and loved Tuesday night training, especially in winter, chasing Tom O'Riordan up Knockmaroon Hill and taking on the best of the Donore crew as we galloped around the Phoenix Park.

In those early days in Tennessee, however, I slogged rather than flowed, and soon my running became more a grind than a joy.

In ways, the Tennessee experience had already begun to spell the end of my career as an elite athlete, but I did not suspect that at the time.

24

Running On Empty

LOOKING back, I realise I beat myself up too much for being a weak link on the team that finished second in the 1972 National Collegiate Cross Country Championships, where Neil Cusack led the field a merry dance to win the individual title.

I threw myself hardly any slack for the fact I was running injured, with little power to push off my right leg. I had expected better of myself and I felt a huge sense of responsibility for our narrow failure to win team gold, though neither the coach nor my team-mates ever chided me for my lowly finish.

On a cool, dry track that day in Houston, Neil Cusack was up front from an early stage, on the heels of the Englishman Nick Rose, who was running for Western Kentucky. Rose led the field through the opening mile, with Cusack just a second adrift and John Hartnett from Cork and Villanova University lying third, a few strides ahead of Eddie Leddy.

As they passed halfway of the six-mile distance, Cusack was in command, and he coasted from there to a brilliant victory. Doug Brown from the University of Tennessee in Knoxville finished second, with Eddie Leddy following fast in third.

Another Irishman, Dan Murphy from Kerry, running for Washington State University, finished a brilliant fifth, and PJ Leddy ran well to place 15th for ETSU, one place ahead of John Hartnett.

The casual spectator might have assumed that, with three runners in the top 15, East Tennessee State were about to wrap up the team title, but it was not to be; when Kevin Breen from Offaly posted a modest 95th and I trailed home 104th, Coach Walker knew the points race for team gold would be a cliffhanger.

Ray McBride, essentially a middle-distance man, was never expected to influence the outcome, and finished 173rd, solid running in the circumstances.

It all came down to Kevin and myself, and when the points were added up they showed that the University of Tennessee had beaten ETSU by just six points.

Had it been any other team in the entire USA that beat us we could have soaked it up and felt great about silver, but to be pipped for glory by our nearest neighbour and arch rival was devastating and took the gloss off what should have been a day of unbridled celebration after Cusack's majestic victory.

For a long time I blamed myself for getting injured in the Regional qualifier, and I also blamed myself for not levelling with Coach Walker about the varicose vein surgery I had undergone just weeks before arriving at ETSU.

I figured if I had told him about those lost weeks of training he might have allowed me ease in more gradually in September. But I feared he would send me right back home if he knew I was less than fully fit, and so I struggled from day one in the hills of East Tennessee.

Years later I would understand when Cusack told me it had taken him a full year to adjust to training twice a day at ETSU. He had arrived on a half scholarship and it took him ages to reach the point where he could match strides with Eddie Leddy, who would run the steeplechase at the 1972 Olympics. Cusack, however, emerged from that year much stronger and qualified to compete in Munich as a team-mate of Leddy.

The two Olympians were in a class apart that season, and Coach Walker had fixed ideas about how close to them Ray McBride and myself needed to be on our daily runs in the mountains.

Walker would record the time gaps between us in cross-country races and demand that we replicated or bettered those deficits each day in the hills. Of course Ray and myself were only adapting to the regime, and the biggest problem was Walker's 'one size fits all' approach — he figured that what was good for two flying Olympians was also good enough for two greenhorns struggling to find their feet.

In some ways he was right but in many ways he was wrong. If you survived the regime, you definitely came out the far end a stronger athlete, but I have always believed I would have run much better on a more gentle introduction to the regime and less training mileage. Of course it's easy to be wise in hindsight.

That day in Houston I had swallowed a handful of painkillers and wore a lumbar heat-pack for sciatica. A week later I dropped out at halfway in the AAU Cross Country Championships in Chicago as my lower back went into brutal spasm.

It was years later that I finally found a cure for what had become recurring sciatic-nerve pain. That was when I visited the chiropractor Ronnie Turner in Dublin. He sorted me out in one session and I wished I had met someone with his skills in East Tennessee all those years before.

When news of the NCAA Cross Country filtered back to Johnson City, the report stated that not only had Neil Cusack taken individual gold but also ETSU had won the team title. Joy was understandably widespread.

It was a bitter pill to swallow for all our loyal fans at ETSU when the bulletin was updated to confirm we had missed out on the title — and to our nearest neighbours — by a mere six points.

Still, we came home to a rapturous welcome and were met at the Tri-Cities airport by the Mayor of Johnson City and the President of ETSU.

In winning individual gold and team silver the Irish Brigade had made cross-country history for the college, and we were treated to a lavish reception attended by a great crowd of fans, among whom many pretty girls were conspicuous by their presence.

Neil Cusack, who with his dark good looks and goatee beard cut a dashing figure, was the hero of the hour. Two years later he would again set pulses racing at ETSU when posting a famous victory in the Boston Marathon.

Cusack, incidentally, would some years later be voted, not once but twice, 'Sexiest Man in Ireland'.

Sadly, my enjoyment of the NCAA aftermath was tinged with bitter disappointment at my own poor showing in the race. I brooded over it for a long time and began to shun company, especially on the days when I felt oppressed by a greyness that even running could not shake off.

It seemed I could not get my tracks in the ground, however hard I tried. I thought about just packing it all in, heading home and not coming back. The brother, Tom, was due home from Australia for Christmas and we had not seen each other for years. That would be a kind of family reunion.

I had one big problem — the piggy-bank was almost empty.

And so on a wing and a prayer I called a priest in New York whose number PJ Leddy had given me. The priest worked for a travel company called St Patrick's Fathers that operated charter flights to Ireland.

I was due some money from the Post Office, maybe just enough to pay for a round trip, and I asked the good priest if there was any way he could give me the ticket on credit.

To my delight the answer was yes — PJ had vouched for me — and soon there was a plane ticket in my mail box, and I stayed true to my promise and paid for it on my return to Tennessee.

I was always glad I made it home then, because we were never subsequently together as complete family at Christmas. Of course I told the folks everything was going swimmingly in Tennessee, even though I was dreading the return trip.

I kept a brave face on things — but already my American dream was beginning to fade.

25

Home For Christmas

I HAVE always been grateful to the those good people in St Patrick's Fathers for advancing me the fare to get home that Christmas of 1972. It's hard to imagine a hard-up student today being the beneficiary of such kindness and trust.

It meant a whole lot to my parents to have Tom and myself under the one roof for a rare Christmas gathering, and it would not have taken much prompting for me to have torn up the return ticket.

I travelled to Limerick on December 30 to celebrate Neil Cusack's birthday and marvelled at the fact that at 21 he was already an Olympian as well as a US Collegiate champion.

Neil had a terrific can-do and full-on attitude to life. Back in Tennessee, it was he who broke the old mould of training built by Coach Walker.

When in the mid-1960s Michael Heery and Patsy Durnin arrived as the first Irish scholarship athletes at ETSU, Walker had them doing six miles, timed, on the track at 6.30 on week mornings. When Cusack arrived he persuaded the coach to change the regime, the early-morning road runs to be easy ones around the campus, and the harder sessions to be long mountain runs, as much as 11 miles, at 3pm.

I recall the afternoon, shortly after we had begun those mountain sessions, when as we headed for the hills I saw Neil fling a pair of light trainers across the perimeter fence and onto the university track. What was he up to, I wondered. I found out later in the afternoon.

Cusack introduced us to a new concept in training — the 11-mile run followed directly by an interval session of ten laps in 67 or 68 seconds with short recovery. I often saw Cusack finish off such sessions with a couple of sub-60 quarters. He was a pure animal to train with.

I had been well used to what I considered hard training with Donore Harriers, and even before I moved to Dublin I was known for my dedication — often getting out three times a day in Ballyhaunis. At one national squad session in Galway, when most of the participants, senior as well as junior, were heading out on the town, I was lacing on the shoes for a late-night run around Salthill.

I never experienced the same joy in training in Tennessee, perhaps because from the start I was playing catch-up and could not mix it as I would have liked with Cusack and Eddie Leddy.

Back home I had been fearless and uninhibited and felt confident of taking on the seniors at every opportunity. I lost some of that youthful exuberance soon after arriving in Tennessee, and something else went out of the day for me when I struggled to the finish that day in Houston, Texas.

I have often wondered what exactly happened to me in ETSU, the place that should have been my ideal proving ground. My form back in Ireland should have been a good enough launch pad to a fine senior career, but it did not happen. Running became more a chore than a joy and I struggled not only physically but also emotionally.

Between the demands of study, hard training and hard dishwashing I was being pulled down. For bad measure, it felt like the 'angel of lonesome' had taken up residence on my shoulder, and the greyness I would later acknowledge as depression became a frequent visitor.

And yet all the time I kept a brave face to the world and pretended I was happy as a piglet in slurry.

26

No Match For Big Bill

I WAS never going to worry my parents by giving them chapter and verse of all the difficulties of my time in East Tennessee, and so there were several adventures and misadventures of which they had to remain blissfully innocent. One such episode was a hair-raising, high-rise and admittedly bizarre run-in with a workmate disappointed with my matchmaking efforts.

During my first two summers at ETSU I worked as a labourer on the Mini-Dome, a huge building project on the campus, something comparable to putting a roof over Croke Park. The finished project would include a raft of sports arenas, including an indoor football field, a six-lane, 280-metre running track and six tennis courts as well as gymnasia and a research lab.

Our foreman was Woodrow Baker, a giant of a man with great heart and attitude.

'Boys,' he would say to us on Monday mornings, 'I just want to see two things from y'all this week — assholes and elbows. So grab them shovels and get moving!'

I enjoyed my time on that site, especially the rich and rare variety of characters I met there, many of them from way back in the hill country.

On the fateful day in question, I was detailed to grease the huge bolts secured to the high walls of the Mini-Dome in preparation for the massive steel roof spans soon to be dropped into place. And so, armed with a big bucket of grease, I was busy at my task, high above the ground, when a workmate I just knew as Bill mounted the scaffold and approached in a manner laced with menace.

I would describe the same Bill as a redneck: a rough diamond in his mid-40s, seldom shaven and often smelling of liquor. I had enjoyed friendly banter with Bill, and he'd often suggested, playfully I thought, that I organise a date for him with one or other of the gorgeous young women over at college. I used to play along, promising to fix him up with his dream date.

This time, however, Bill was far from playful. Reeking of alcohol and stale breath, his face contorted with anger, he leaned toward me and growled in a deep hillbilly drawl right out of the film *Deliverance*.

'I'm disappointed in you, little Irishman. You goddam sonofabitch! You keep tellin' me you'll find me a nice little gal over there but you're just bullshittin' all the time!'

I knew immediately I was in danger. The hair stood on the nape of my neck and my legs were trembling. It was then in confusion that I blurted exactly what he did not want to hear.

'Ah, Bill, maybe you're just past it anyway,' I laughed nervously.

'You no-good sonofabitch!' he roared. 'I'd like you to have a good look now at your hands, because where you're goin' it's the last time you'll be seein' them!'

I glanced down at my hands and of course saw they were covered in grease.

'Have a good look down at the ground while you are at it!' he continued, still eyeball to eyeball with me. 'That's where you're headed when you have a little accident. Just one little nudge from me now and you're not goin' to be able to hold on to nothin' up here to save yourself, are you? You've led me on, you sonofabitch! You were never goin' to fix me up with one of those sweet little college gals.'

I backed away from the crazy man but he kept closing the space, his eyes ablaze with fury. Badly exposed on scaffold planks 100 feet in the air, I kept backpedalling at speed until from the corner of my eye I spotted a ladder that led to the lower levels.

In blind panic I dived for the ladder and hardly hit a rung as I slid down on greased hands to safety. I plunged down several more ladders before finally hitting ground level and, badly shaken and in tears, hurried in search of Woodrow Baker to tell him of my narrow escape.

'Goddam, boy!' Woodrow said. 'You don't want to mess with ol' Bill! Do you not know he's done time in the Penitentiary for shootin' an old boy? That's the type of guy you're dealing with. So I'm going to have a word with him and you, you crazy Irishman, are working here on the ground from now on.'

I never again laboured alongside Bill — my good friend Woodrow kept us well apart — but I often thought of how it would have hit my parents to hear I'd had an 'accident' on that building site in faraway Johnson City, Tennessee. Had I not been fast on my feet that day, I have no doubt the lovelorn Bill would have 'nudged' me to my death.

I would have a few more hairy moments during my time in Tennessee, including the night another man disappointed in love came with his six-shooter loaded and cocked to the dormitory I shared with Eddie Leddy and Ray McBride.

On that occasion straight out of the Wild West I owed my survival to an accident of timing and to the cool head and heroism of a team-mate.

27

Woodrow And The Ape

I ENJOYED my time working with Woodrow Baker and his construction crew on the building of the Mini-Dome, and it was great to watch, up close and personal, the huge building take shape.

To get a job on the site my first summer in Tennessee was a heavensend; I was flat broke with no hope of getting the money together to fly home for a few weeks' holidays and a visit to my parents.

The June afternoon college broke up for the summer, I watched as students packed their belongings and the huge car park near our dormitory gradually emptied out. I was now on my own; all the students and faculty had gone their separate ways, and even my team-mates on the Irish Brigade had been able to escape Johnson City.

My best pal, Ray McBride, was, like myself, unable to afford the trip back to Ireland, but he was lucky in that an aunt had invited him to stay with her in New Jersey for the summer.

Our student quarters were close to the railroad track near Johnson City, and that night the wail of the whistle and sound of the bell as the freight trains passed stirred up the homesickness in me as never before. And so I paced the dormitory, listening to the high, lonesome sound from the track and wondering how I would survive the summer.

The first time I met Woodrow Baker we hit it off. Woodrow had a busted nose that had never properly set, and the story was that while drunk at the County Fair he had entered a cage to wrestle a trained gorilla.

The challenge was to last five minutes with the gorilla and win 100 dollars, but it was impossible to get a grip on the great beast — the circus people had him greased all over.

Unable to get a handhold, ol' Woodrow soon got frustrated and hit his opponent with a haymaker to the midriff — only to receive a slap back that broke his nose and landed him on his back. Woodrow never got the nose set and it became something of a badge of honour and the stuff of legend.

Woodrow was a hard but fair taskmaster and had assembled a great team around him. He had little formal education but could pinpoint and solve construction problems quicker than the highly qualified engineers and architects on site. He had natural talent and common sense and commanded respect from every member of his crew.

When the massive support walls of concrete were being poured, Woodrow deployed me to a big vibrator, making sure the hot concrete was spread evenly around and inside the huge steel support forms.

Because I was small and wiry I could easily get into tight areas between the forms, but it was hard and dangerous work. The big crane bucket would swing overhead and deposit its load of concrete within inches of where I worked the vibrator, and every couple of hours I would have to leave my perch for a quick shower and complete change of clothes.

I had no fear of heights and later on worked high up on the scaffolds vibrating concrete and helping the steelworkers.

In the evenings, when work was over, I would often join Woodrow and his men for beers in a local bar. They were a colourful crew, and I loved to observe their zest for life and living. They could be rough, especially when the beer was flowing, but if you earned their friendship they would always watch your back.

The only men on his crew Woodrow disliked were certain football players, or 'jocks', privileged students on football scholarships, and there were two in particular he objected to —

smart-asses who arrived mornings on site in flashy sportscars, strutted around like primadonnas and invested more energy in dodging work than doing it.

There were days on site when it rained and work had to be abandoned, and on those days we would huddle in huts and wait for the rain to clear. If someone happened by on such days and asked Woodrow how things were going, his answer was usually, 'Hell, we're just kickin' a dawg today.' I don't know where the saying originated, but it was his way of saying that work was suspended.

One day in high summer Woodrow went looking for his two 'jocks' after they failed to complete a task he had set them. He eventually found them lying in a secluded spot on a quiet corner of the site, sound asleep with their folded tee-shirts acting as pillows.

Woodrow lost it and drew a few kicks on the sleeping figures. 'What in hell do you boys think you're doing?' he bellowed.

Now wide awake and on their feet, the jocks were at first stuck for words until Jack, the one who was always the loudest, quipped, 'Ah, Woodrow, calm down! Don't you see we're just kickin' a dawg?'

'Boy,' Woodrow replied, 'What you just said has landed you with one big problem.'

'What's that?' asked Jack, now a little chastened.

'Well, boy,' Woodrow said in his slow and measured drawl, 'the big problem is you were trying to act smart at my expense with your "just kickin' a dawg".'

'Hell, Woodrow, can't you take a joke and give us a break?' Jack said.

'You're missin' the point, boy,' Woodrow replied. 'The big problem with you kickin' a dawg is that I'm the dawg. Now go get your things and whatever money you're due and get your useless ass the hell off my site!'

Woodrow was a real hillbilly in the best sense of the word, and there were evenings when after work on the site I should have gone out training but opted instead to share a pitcher of beer with the man who wrestled the gorilla.

There was a day too when Woodrow took me to a farm for a stint at cutting tobacco. That day had a rowdy ending in a rough honky-tonk that earned me a bunch of cracked ribs and a lot of deep bruising.

Bad timing too — only a few weeks before college regrouped for the fall semester and of course the cross-country season. But that sort of mistiming would become a feature of my scholarship career.

28

Ray Of Sunshine

I HAD a bad clash with Coach Walker in the summer of 1973, after my first year at ETSU.

That first year had ended in frustration. I had qualified to run in the National Collegiate Track and Field Championships, but Walker dropped me from the team. Feeling I had done enough to justify my inclusion, I wondered if his decision was some kind of payback for my disappointing run in the NCAA Cross Country the previous autumn, when the Irish Brigade missed out on team gold by an agonising few points.

I had given it my best shot that day in Houston, considering I was drugged up on painkillers for sciatica and ran with a heat pack on my lower back — all the legacy of an injury sustained at the Conference Cross Country, the qualifier race for the Nationals.

I had run a storming last lap at the Conference, gaining vital points for the team, but nearing the finish did some damage to the sciatic nerve — an injury that would plague me for years.

Coach Walker was yelling loudly at me that day as I headed out on the last lap in Bloomington, Indiana. His message was neither polite nor politically correct, but it spurred me into overdrive and I picked off four opponents to garner the points needed for team victory.

When I crossed the line, that bear of a man grabbed me, lifted me off my feet and hugged and shook me for what seemed an eternity, because all the while my right spike was gouging my left foot as I struggled to untangle the legs.

I survived the crush and emerged bloodied but ecstatic to join the lads in celebration. It was next morning that I knew I was in trouble when I struggled to drive off the right leg.

That day at the qualifier race I was curious as to why winning the team title was such a big deal for Coach Walker. Then Eddie Leddy explained that the Conference title was the one guarantee the coach's contract would be renewed for another year; team victory was his meal ticket.

In those days, the Tennessee sports bulletins regularly carried news of the sacking of college football, basketball, baseball and track coaches across the state. A coach was measured, with little sentiment, by the success of his team. I suspect there is even less sentiment today.

Walker was up front about such pressures, and though during my time at ETSU we disagreed on many things, deep down I greatly respected the man I always addressed as Coach. We were never as close as that day when he hugged me in Indiana, and it took a lot of years after I finished up in Tennessee for us to make peace and bury the hatchet.

I was feeling hard done by at the end of that first year in College. Years later I recognised that my difficulties with Walker masked the real issues — I was desperately lonely and depressed. I found the perfect opportunity to lash back at Coach Walker when at the end of that first year he threatened to cut Ray McBride's scholarship over a misdemeanour that seemed to me far from serious.

Like myself, Ray found that first year in Tennessee extremely tough, and for him there was the added difficulty that he was a middle- rather than long-distance specialist; his preferred races were 800 metres and steeplechase.

Following the threat of suspension, Ray went to stay with an aunt in New Jersey for the summer and I donned my hard hat and headed for the construction site over at the Mini-Dome. But I reckon if we'd had the funds we might both have returned to Ireland and called it a day.

With possible suspension looming, Ray was understandably distraught, and after he headed to New Jersey I confronted Walker and told him that if he was going to drop my best friend from the team he could also forget about having me on the Irish Brigade for the fall of 1973.

Come fall, the stalemate persisted. The Irish Brigade had regrouped but I was still vibrating concrete high up on the Mini-Dome. McBride had returned to campus with faint hope that Walker would relent and renew his scholarship and I had given my ultimatum: bring McBride back or lose both of us.

Of course I knew I was holding a trump card. Coach Walker needed a full cross-country team, especially after our team silver medal of the previous season in Houston. He needed me on board as a scoring member, and I was willing to gamble that he would relent and give my friend back his scholarship. At the same time I was prepared to accept the consequences of my action — if it failed, I would work a few more months on the Mini-Dome and then head back home.

For a week I watched from my perch high on the scaffold as Neil Cusack and Eddie Leddy led the cross-country team out toward the mountains for afternoon training. And each day when Coach Walker looked up from his support car as they passed close to the Mini-Dome, I took off my hard hat and waved it at him in defiance.

And then into the second week the summons came; a messenger arrived on the site with an urgent request that I visit Coach Walker in his office. The meeting was short and to the point.

'You know that you have me over a barrel and I need you to run for me this fall,' Walker said. 'I'm not going to fight you any more on this but I won't forget the position you're putting me in.'

'I'm only standing up for my friend,' I replied.

'Listen,' Walker said, 'I want you to take off that silly hard hat right now and throw it in the bin. I then want you to go back to the site and tell your foreman you're quitting. And I further want you to be present here for training at three sharp this afternoon.'

'Does that mean McBride gets to train too?' I enquired.

'Don't push your luck,' Walker said. 'If he's back on campus — as I'm told he is — you can tell McBride to get his sorry ass ready for practice as well.

'Now get out of here and don't ever pull something like this on me again or, I promise, you'll regret it.'

'See you at training, Coach,' I said as I bounded out of the office and headed off to find McBride and tell him the good news.

During our second year at ETSU Ray decided to change his major from Business Studies to Theatre and that came about almost by accident. I was pursuing a major in Theatre — that I later changed to journalism — and one of the course requirements was that I direct a one-act play.

I chose *Riders to the Sea* by John Millington Synge and cast Ray in the lead role, Bartley. *Riders to the Sea* is a beautiful play. I was lucky in the cast I assembled, the production got great reviews, and for several nights the 'sold out' sign went up.

The night of the finale, Ray and myself went for a few beers to our local, Sammy's Apex, and it was there that Ray announced his decision to change course.

'Feck it, Greally,' he said, 'I don't want to spend my life in an office in Galway "fumbling in the greasy till". You're after getting me hooked on acting and I want to be a professional. I'm changing my major and that's it!'

Ray went on to become a brilliant actor and the year he graduated from ETSU he was cast in the lead role in a professional production of *The Playboy of the Western World*, another gem from the pen of Synge.

That production ran for the summer in the famous Barter Theatre in Abingdon, Virginia, where during the Great Depression actors from Broadway used to arrive to tread the boards in return for food and lodgings.

Ray's Christy Mahon won rave reviews and proved a stepping

stone to success in the Druid and Abbey theatres as well as films including *Into the West* and *Reefer and the Model*.

And then, approaching the pinnacle of his acting career, tragedy struck when Ray was diagnosed with a cancer that affected his speech and balance. For a lad who could talk, sing, dance and run for Ireland — and indeed did so on all four counts — it was a terrible blow.

The great American wordsmith Thomas Wolfe was on the money when he wrote in *You Can't Go Home Again* that there is no going 'back to youth and that wonderful feeling of invincibility'.

In recent times I have thought a lot about those words, especially while out running. And they have brought me back more than a decade to a few lines I wrote in haste one night after visiting Ray in hospital. This was my Song for Ray:

We were young and thought we would never die;
You had the look of invincibility in your eye;
And there wasn't much that we wouldn't try,
In the glory days back then.

And I remember a day down at Shannonside,
And your family there all filled with pride,
As you and I left for Tennessee;
That was a glory day back then.

But tonight I saw you in a hospital bed,
So weak you could hardly lift your head,
And you turned to me and smiled and said,
Where do all the good times go?

And does anyone know where those good times go;
If you do, please tell me, because I want to know,
For I've had my share and I'd like to find,
Where those good times are all stored.

Yes we were young and thought we would never die;
You had that look of invincibility in your eye;
And there wasn't much that we wouldn't try,
In the glory days back then.

The years go by and the memories endure;
Yes, we had our good times, and that's for sure;
And we lived in the day and knew no fear,
In the glory days back then.

But the years are creeping up on you and me,
And life has changed from what it used to be,
In those carefree days in East Tennessee;
Those were glory days back then.

We were young and thought we would never die;
You had the look of invincibility in your eye;
And there wasn't much that we wouldn't try,
In the glory days back then.

When I visit Ray now at his home in the Claddagh we talk and remember glory days in Tennessee — and indeed there are times when for long spells we say nothing at all, just sitting together quietly, two lifelong pals in silent harmony.

29

Beauty And The Beast

EVEN when things were going badly pear-shaped for me in Johnson City, my letters home always accentuated the positive — to hint at problems, not to mention the several serious scrapes I got myself into, would have been to compound for my parents the pain and worry of separation.

One of the close shaves I did not write home about was when Paul, a fellow I barely knew, turned up armed and dangerous at Cooper Hall to visit me in the dorm room I shared with Eddie Leddy and Ray McBride.

Eddie arrived back from an evening study session in the Campus Library to find the would-be hitman, highly agitated, pacing up and down the hall by our door and checking and rechecking a loaded handgun.

Two months earlier Paul had been introduced by Eddie to Ray and myself. He could have been Irish with his flaming red hair and pale, freckled face, but he turned out to be a rowdy redneck who had for a while worked shifts with Eddie in the dish-room at the campus cafeteria.

The night Paul was introduced to us he joined our party and accompanied us to a bar to meet some girls. As the evening gathered energy, Paul took a big shine to Linda, a good friend of mine and a real beauty. He somehow ended up getting a date with her for the following week, but it was a short-lived flirtation and after that Linda did not want to see him again despite his daily phonecalls to her.

In the meantime, I went out with Linda a few times — nothing serious, just trips to the movies and to a local bar. Little did I suspect that Paul was watching our every move, all the while getting more jealous and more obsessed.

Than one Sunday evening Paul and one of his redneck friends arrived on campus and offered to drive Ray and myself to Bristol, Virginia, to buy some beer. You could not purchase beer or liquor in Johnson City on a Sunday, and so we often travelled — religiously you might say — on a Sabbath beer run about 30 minutes across the Tennessee border.

On the trip to Bristol, Paul and his friend were super friendly with us, but on the return journey to Johnson City, the mood in the car suddenly changed; the talking stopped, the whole dynamic flipped, and as we exchanged glances in the back seat Ray and I sensed something bad was afoot.

Our fears were confirmed when the car picked up speed and after a few miles suddenly careered off the main highway down a narrow, winding road. And all the time Paul was leering at his pal in the passenger seat, a crazy, manic grin.

The car eventually skidded to a halt at the edge of a lake, but when Paul noticed a courting couple in a car nearby he abruptly spun the wheel and sped back toward campus. Not a word was spoken on that return journey and when we arrived at college we just grabbed our six-packs and bolted to our room.

Ray and myself always believed that but for the courting couple that beer run might have ended very badly indeed. We reckoned the two good ol' boys meant to do us harm, and when Paul spun the car back toward the highway we felt overwhelming relief.

It was two weeks later that Paul arrived outside our door with his loaded handgun.

'Where the hell is Greally?' he snarled at Eddie. 'I'm going to shoot his bad ass because he's messed me around with that woman!'

Eddie kept his cool and displayed wonderful presence of mind by inviting the agitated gunman into the room to air his grievances. It took Eddie two hours, but he managed to talk Paul into leaving the gun back in the car and returning for a chat while awaiting my arrival.

I arrived back presently after being out on the town with the lovely Linda and rambled into the room to find Paul sitting high up on Ray McBride's bunk bed and talking rapidly to Eddie, who was sitting on my bed.

'What's happening, guys?' I hollered in friendly greeting.

Paul glared down at me: 'Where have you been, boy?'

'Hell, Paul, I've just been down town with that ol' gal Linda that you took out a few weeks ago. You missed the boat there, man — she's a real cracker!'

With that, Paul sprang down from the bunk and in one quick movement slapped me viciously against the wall.

'I came here to kill you tonight and now I have damn good reason!' he roared, squeezing me hard by the throat.

Luckily for me, Eddie was quick into action and managed to pull Paul away while screaming at me: 'Frank, this is no joke! Stop messing and listen!'

I was winded and scared and I knew Eddie was deadly serious.

'It's a big misunderstanding, Paul, and you need to calm down!' Eddie roared. 'Frank just happened to go out with Linda tonight, with no agenda.

'Paul, we've been friends for a long time and I give you my word we'll not take this any further if you leave now. Otherwise I'll call the Campus Police, and no woman is worth getting yourself locked up for.'

As Paul seemed to waver, Eddie continued with impressive steel in his voice: 'I want you to shake hands with Frank and myself and call a truce. We've done you no wrong and I believe you're an honourable guy.'

Eddie Leddy stood tall that night and managed to stamp his authority on a highly volatile situation.

'Leave it and end it now and let's have those handshakes,' he persisted.

To my astonishment and relief, Paul reached for my hand and grabbed it tightly: 'I still think you're one sonofabitch, Greally, and you better be glad it was Eddie I met when I arrived here tonight.'

'We'll leave it at that,' I said, with all the composure I could muster.

Eddie and myself watched from the window as Paul walked across the carpark.

'What if he changes his mind and comes back with the gun?' I asked.

'If he does, we may both be in trouble,' Eddie laughed nervously.

'Frank,' he said as I hugged him, 'I don't think you'll ever fully realise how close you came to being blown away tonight. You cannot joke with people like Paul — he was crazy enough to kill you.'

We looked out the window again and Paul's car was still there in the parking lot. Then we saw the headlights come on and we watched as he spun the car in a tight arc and sped away.

'You'll have a cup of tea,' I said as reality set in and my legs started to shake.

'Yes,' Eddie said. 'I feel like I have at least earned that tonight. Put on the kettle, Frank.'

30

Runner's High

THE only time I ran when on drugs was a scary night in 1975 when my drink was spiked with a hit of LSD. Of course I had competed in the 1972 NCAA Cross Country after swallowing a handful of painkillers for sciatica, but the LSD experience was unintentional and one I would never like to repeat.

It was at a weekend party that someone slipped the hallucinogenic drug into my drink and the result was pretty immediate. The party was in full swing when I made my exit through a first-floor window, dropped to the ground and sprinted up the road with a number of partygoers who had witnessed my transformation and unorthodox exit in hot pursuit.

I remember that in the madness of the moment I imagined I was Ronnie Delany and the feeling was definitely an out-of-body one.

This time, with the LSD boost, there was no catching me as I hurtled into the night, and so everyone returned to partying, hoping I would find my way back to campus.

I still remember parts of that night, especially my determination to head out to the highway and run full tilt at one of the big trucks in full flight. I believed such were my powers that, Superman-like, I could stop one of those speeding monsters in its tracks.

Fortunately, I never made it to the highway. Later, recalling fragments of the nightmarish episode, I could only conclude that I spent several hours going around in circles — missing the route to the highway every time. All I know for sure is that I eventually woke up in bright daylight, in the front seat of a dump-truck on a construction site, from where I could hear the traffic whizzing past on the nearby highway.

I lay there trying to get my bearings and put the events of the night into some kind of order, but the harder I tried the more I struggled. I was not even sure what day it was, but I presumed that because there was nobody on the site it had to be Sunday.

My clothes were covered in cement dust, and I guessed that after staggering around for a time I had stumbled into the dump truck and fallen asleep.

I dusted myself off and slowly made my way toward the highway that led to Johnson City, hoping to hitch a ride back to college. I had wandered for several hours and was swaying there on the hard shoulder when a small, colourful bus straight out of Hippieland pulled in and, with a whoosh of air, two doors opened.

I recognised the driver; Seamus Hemingway was an art teacher back at college and someone with whom I had shared a few drinks in Sammy's Apex. It was getting dusk by now, and as he peered at me in the half light, I could see Seamus register astonishment.

'Frank! What the hell are you doing out here and what's happening?'

'I'm heading back to college, Seamus, if you could take me there,' I replied as if out for a routine stroll.

'My question is where are you coming from at this time of evening — it looks like you've been rolling in concrete.'

'It's a long story,' I replied, 'and I'm too tired to even start telling you, Seamus.'

I sat back on a front seat of the bus, and across the way were two wide-eyed and open-mouthed kids — a boy and a girl — staring at me as if they had seen a ghost.

I took a few deep breaths, gathered my thoughts as best I could and enquired of Seamus, 'Can you please tell me what time of day it is?'

'It's almost seven o'clock, Frank.'

I pondered that reply before broaching another question: 'I hope you don't mind me asking, but can you tell me what day it is?'

'Hey, you're really far out, Man!' Seamus replied. 'It's Sunday evening of course. Wherever you're coming from, there must have been one hell of a party!'

Seamus dropped me off near the campus and, still shaky on my feet and ravenous with hunger, I headed up toward the dormitories and apartment buildings. It was then I met the search party headed by Neil Cusack and just returning from an afternoon manhunt all over Johnson City.

It seemed word of my breakout and disappearance had reached campus, and friends got worried when I failed to show up by Sunday midday. Of course, they berated me for my idiocy, but I was still much too strung out to take notice.

Their anger softened when a few days later we found out what had triggered the insanity. A soldier lately back from the Vietnam War had spiked my drink and thought it hilarious to see me disappear out a window.

At the time, I hung out a bit with some of those war 'veterans' — young men going back to college on the GI Bill, trying as best they could to get back to education but many finding solace in drink and drugs as a way to blot out the trauma they had endured in Vietnam.

I soon found out the identity of the LSD prankster — and from then on I kept a safe distance from him and his buddies.

31

Drowning Not Waving

I OFTEN think about how close I came to drowning in Boone Lake, East Tennessee, and taking at least one other person down with me as well.

It was the summer of 1976 and I was enjoying a very laid back weekend out at the lake in the company of Lisa, my girlfriend at the time, and her best friend, Bobbie.

After working a shift in the Midtown Inn down in Johnson City, I had arrived back on campus that Friday to find a note pinned to the door of the apartment I shared, temporarily, with Ray Flynn and Louis Kenny. It was an invitation to join Lisa at her brother's house near the lake — he would be out of town for the weekend, giving us free range of the house and a barge that would allow us to go floating on the water.

Of course it was an invitation I could not turn down, and shortly after phoning her, I saw Lisa drive into the parking lot below.

'It's going to be a real fun weekend,' my high-spirited and bubbly friend assured me. And so, after picking up supplies of beer and food, we headed out of the city.

The house near the lake was spacious and for good measure the sun beamed from a clear, blue sky. It was going to be an idyllic weekend, I thought — and for the most part it was.

On the Friday night as we were enjoying the sunset over the lake, Lisa decided to invite her friend Bobbie, as well as Bobbie's boyfriend, to join us the following day for a punt around the lake. It seemed a good idea and we were all set for an early start on Saturday when Bobbie arrived alone. I never found out what happened to her boyfriend but he was a no-show that morning.

It was another heaven-sent day, and before long we had dropped anchor in a secluded cove — an idyllic spot for a picnic and for sunbathing while also enjoying a few beers and a little tequila too. All in all, it was one of those perfect days when all is right with the world and you think you have it made.

Presently, Lisa suggested we go for a swim. Of course I had to sheepishly confess that my only stroke was the anchor stroke and that since almost drowning in a boghole back in Ballyhaunis years earlier I had developed a terror of water. The girls, however, would have none of it; they kept teasing and cajoling me to join them, promising they would keep me safe and soon have me swimming like a dolphin.

I gave in when Lisa produced a set of floats from the barge. There were floats for my arms, body and legs, and with a few beers under my belt I felt almost courageous as Lisa and Bobbie prepared me for what they promised would be a 'floating experience'.

I soon got to like the feeling of floating safely on the water — closely guarded by these two real beauties — and all went swimmingly until Lisa and Bobbie started to gradually remove my supports.

I felt okay when the first floats were taken off, but when the fun-loving girls relieved me of the remaining ones I went into a blind panic, grabbed Lisa, who was nearest to me, and brought her with me, kicking and flailing, under the water.

Lisa would later tell me I had latched onto her with a deadman's grip that she could not shake off. I have no doubt that had we been alone on the lake both of us would have drowned.

I will never know how we resurfaced from the depths, but when we did, Bobbie, who had some lifeguard experience, hit me a ferocious slap on the face that stunned me long enough for her to get me to the barge. Then she had to go back and attend to Lisa, still in distress after her underwater ordeal.

It took me a long time to regain composure, and my two lady friends were also in lingering shock. Especially frightening was the full realisation of how isolated we were in that secluded cove, with no other possible help at hand.

I suspect if I had clamped a drowning man's grip on both my lovely friends that day the story would have had a tragic ending, and I often wonder what they would have made of it at home if the message came through that Frank had drowned in Boone Lake with two young women.

I never gained confidence enough to learn to swim. I think two close calls were enough for me — a third might not have been so lucky.

32

A Different Drum

AS the moment of truth came ever closer, I wondered how my parents would have felt the previous September had they suspected the challenges I was about to face during my final year in Tennessee. Or did they, in fact, have an inkling that all was not as it should be?

They knew me well enough. Surely, when it came time for me to head out the door for Ballyhaunis rail station — leaving them lonesome again — there was something in my gung-ho demeanour that rang false. Perhaps they sensed that all was not was it should be but, like me, were unwilling or unable to face the hard reality.

It never got easy leaving my parents, but this time I was at least able to remind them that in 12 months' time I would be back home for good. And of course they wanted to know, as always, if I was okay for funds. And, as usual, I told them that I was fine and still had plenty of dollars for the journey.

My mother kept telling me — and maybe it was to convince herself — that I would soon be conferred with my degree. And I had not the heart to mention the conversation I'd had with Coach Walker after the last track meet of the season.

This was the end of my third year at ETSU and my racing form had been dismal. And as was usual at the end of the season, as the team bus brought us back to campus, we athletes were called up in turn to the front to sit with Coach Walker and hear his analysis of our year. I had been dreading this evaluation because I knew the proverbial writing was on the wall for me.

Sure enough, Walker came straight to the point. He had given me enough chances to deliver on the track and he rightly sensed that my heart was just not in it any more. I was marching to a different drum, hanging out with writers, artists and musicians, writing poems and songs — all in a vain attempt to avoid facing what was really happening to me.

I was achieving a modicum of success with some of my efforts, winning prizes for ballads I had penned and seeing them in print in college publications. I had wanted to write ever since first delving into Grandfather Mannion's library back in Drimbane, and I now felt I was finding some sort of niche — even if it wasn't in running.

I was skipping classes too and had opted out of required courses in maths and biology because I doubted my ability to cope with them — signing up instead for lectures, many of them extracurricular, in subjects close to my heart: journalism, English literature, creative writing. In those subjects I took classes far in excess of the number required to complete my degree.

I had become enthralled by some of the great American writers, especially Southerners such as Thomas Wolfe, William Faulkner, James Agee and Sherwood Anderson. And we had a wonderful English teacher in Dave McClellan, a man of rare genius who brought literature to life in the classroom.

When McClellan took me to visit the poet and novelist James Dickey in the Martha Washington Hotel in Abingdon, Virginia, I felt I had been accepted into the pantheon.

That evening I sat spellbound as Dickey read his poems as well as passages from *Deliverance*, the widely acclaimed novel of his that had inspired the powerful film of the same title.

Before the reading, Dickey had entertained us in his room, grinning boozily as he played his 12-string guitar, pausing now and then to pour generous measures from a Jeroboam of Jim Bean bourbon before eventually launching into his own rendition of *Duelling Banjos*, the haunting and hair-raising tune from *Deliverance* the film.

Dave McClellan had studied creative writing under Dickey at the University of South Carolina and used to regale us students with stories of Dickey's outrageous behaviour and larger-than-life persona.

I would sneak into McClellan's evening lectures just to hear the great professor deliver rare insights into the lives and works of my heroes, including the Beat poets and writers Jack Kerouac and Allen Ginsberg. After those night classes, we would sometimes stand for an hour or more outside, under the stars, myself and my teacher, talking of literature and life.

Perverse as it may seem, when I heard Professor McClellan relate how many of the great writers had suffered from depression I found comfort in that. At the same time I was also finding comfort in alcohol, and Coach Walker was well aware of my all-too-frequent visits to Sammy's Apex.

I was also desperately lonely and homesick, but that too was something I refused to talk about. Of course I was neglecting the one thing that might have saved me — my running — and I had run out of road as far as my scholarship was concerned.

And so I had left Ballyhaunis again on that September day in 1975 with little more than the train fare to Dublin and my return ticket to New York. I did not even have the air fare from New York to Tennessee — I had given my remaining dollars to a great friend and character, a Texan, who had come to visit me while I was home on holidays.

Benny Patrick assured me he would repay the loan by leaving the cheque with a friend in New York for collection by me en route to Johnson City. And so I boarded the plane in Dublin more in hope than expectation that the bold Benny would not let me down.

I ended up travelling south to Tennessee on a Trailways bus.

33

Slow Coach To Nowhere

BENNY PATRICK was a native of the Lone Star State and as wild as the West Texas wind. We met at one of Dave McClellan's Literature classes, became bosom buddies and hung out together on weekends, mostly on Saturday nights when Benny had finished his shift as a reporter for the *Johnson City Press Chronicle*.

Benny was a tall, rugged and sometimes very loud Texan who was also brilliantly gifted. He had made his mark as an investigative reporter for the *Chronicle* and was an award-winning photographer and creative writer, an expert gunsmith and an acknowledged authority on the construction and workings of Volkswagen engines. He could build musical instruments — guitars and hammer dulcimers — and to ice the whole extravagant cake he could play a mean guitar.

On Saturday nights Benny would come by the university campus with a case of beer in tow. His favourite word was 'fan-tas-tic' and he employed it repeatedly in his deep Texas drawl. He knew plenty about what it was like to feel lonely and isolated, but he hid it well under a full-on approach to life, giving everyone the impression he was always feeling 'fan-tas-tic'.

Benny was the first person I told about my depression and he instantly understood. We would talk all night about books and music and the human condition. We would travel deep into the mountains, visiting strange and wonderful characters he had befriended. There would be music and song and more often than not a jar or three of moonshine.

We knew a lot about core loneliness, Benny and I, and these forays into the hills were balm for both of us.

At the end of my third year at ETSU Benny decided to make a summer trip to Ireland and hook up with me in Ballyhaunis. For good measure, he did the grand tour, visiting Ray McBride in Galway, Eddie and PJ Leddy in Leitrim and Neil Cusack in Limerick. As he often said, the whole trip was 'fan-tas-tic'.

Then when it was time to return home he found he was running short of dollars, and of course I gave him most of what I had in hand — including the fare for my flight from New York to Tennessee that I had yet to book. No problem; Benny would leave a cheque for me with a journalist friend in New York.

And so I flew out of Dublin Airport on a September morning in 1975 with 20 dollars in my pocket. I was going back to nothing, because my scholarship had been pulled. I had thought of coming clean and telling my parents, but something was holding me back and I had sallied forth again full of cheery words and feigned optimism.

It was with some trepidation that I lifted the phone at Kennedy Airport to dial the number Benny had scribbled. When it came to financial matters, Benny was a bit like myself: the money just flowed in and out. I wondered if he had left the cheque as promised, and if so would there be enough in it to book a ticket from La Guardia to Tri-Cities in Tennessee.

It was reassuring to hear a pleasant female voice at the other end of the line. Mike's wife told me her husband was at work in the city but would be home before midnight. I enquired if Benny had visited and she told me yes, he had stayed a few days in New York and he and her husband had hit the town pretty hard. I timidly enquired if Benny had left a cheque but she couldn't say — I would have to call Mike.

'Hell, old Benny sure left a cheque for you all right,' Mike told me when he answered the phone at the radio station where he worked as a news journalist. 'But you know the way it is with Benny

— I'll need to clear it with the bank before I can give you the money. Why don't you come out to Queens and stay the night and we can go to the bank in the morning?'

I hadn't a clue where Queens was but I jotted down the address and told Mike I was heading there.

'See you around midnight,' he said and hung up.

How I eventually got to the New York Borough of Queens and found the address I'm not sure. But I made it there, dog-tired, hungry and thirsty, and I was greeted like a long-lost friend by Mike's wife.

'Would you like something to eat?' she asked. Despite the fact I was now ready to devour a table leg, I politely declined — hoping of course that, as was the custom back home, the invitation would be repeated with growing insistence until I had no option but to relent.

'How about a beer then?' she asked.

I grabbed the proffered can of beer with both hands and for the next three hours we made small talk and watched TV as the hunger pangs intensified and we awaited her husband's arrival.

When Mike finally returned he tossed me another beer and I heard him ask his wife in the kitchen if the little Irishman had eaten.

'I did ask him, Mike, but he told me he was okay and I didn't press him.'

I resolved there and then it was the last time I would ever refuse a bite to eat. The hunger knocks lingered all through that long night in Queens as I tossed and turned and tried to find merciful sleep.

The following morning Mike took me to the bank and produced the precious cheque. To my dismay it was a good few dollars short of what I had expected — but at least it cleared the system and it was reassuring to feel cash in my hand again. There was insufficient, however, for an air ticket to Tri-Cities and I was reluctant to ask Mike — for all his and his wife's warm hospitality to a virtual stranger — for a temporary bail-out.

'I'll drive you to La Guardia,' he said.

Quick as a flash the answer came to me: 'I'll tell you what, Mike, I think I'll go by bus. Can you take me to the Trailways bus depot?'

'Are you crazy, Frank?' he said. 'It'll take you days to get to Tennessee on one of those buses!'

'I'm in no hurry, and anyway I've always wanted to do that trip by bus,' I lied.

We shook hands at the Port Authority in Manhattan, where to my extreme relief I found I had enough for the busfare as well as a few dollars more for food.

We took almost two full days to reach Johnson City, and when I arrived on campus I was greeted by Tommy McCormack, who told me he had some good news and some bad news.

The good news was he had organised a job for me in the cafeteria dish-room and the bad news was that all his efforts to persuade Coach Walker to put me back on scholarship had fallen on deaf ears.

'Walker is not for turning,' Tommy said. 'This time it's for real and you're out. Here's 50 dollars to tide you over for a few days.'

Tommy told me Louis Kenny and Ray Flynn were offering me floor space to lay my sleeping bag until I could find something better — and then he added a health warning: 'Now don't you be going off to Sammy's Apex to spend that money, Frank! Get some solid food into you and things will work out okay!'

I thanked Tommy for his generosity and went to deposit my few bags in the dormitory room of Louis and Ray.

I was heartsick and weary and I felt there was only one place I could find temporary refuge and comfort — the high stool and the bright lights at Sammy's Apex. I pulled on my jacket and headed there.

34

Home At Last

I ASKED the bus driver to drop me off at the spring well, about 300 yards from the old homestead in Devlis. From there I could see the house and the smoke rising from the chimney — and again I was overwhelmed by a sense of guilt and failure.

I was arriving home with little to show from my four years in Tennessee but a few small presents and souvenirs, and I wondered how the folks would react on seeing me arrive at the door unannounced and, just as worrying, how I would explain myself.

The memory came back of an evening when I was about 10. It was the fateful day when my mother presented me with a freshly strung fiddle — an heirloom passed down from my grandfather Harry Mannion and lovingly restored at great expense — and invited me to play for my father and herself the few tunes I had learned of late.

I had supposedly been attending lessons in Ballyhaunis for six months, lessons that were costing my parents the not inconsiderable weekly sum of half a crown. But after half-a-dozen classes I had opted out, heading to the public library when I was supposed to be taking instruction, and squirrelling my mother's hard-saved money away to be spent on Sundays at the pictures, whether in the Parochial Hall or the Star Cinema.

Leo Byrne was a very accomplished man, a good teacher and also a noted bandleader. But I never felt comfortable with him, and I suppose that was because he tried his best to impose some kind of structure on me, and so I rebelled.

And of course, in the very same pattern of evasion I would bring to a fine art in Tennessee, I kept assuring my mother all was well and I was learning lots of fine tunes under Leo's tutelage.

I got a terrible shock when my mother proudly produced the beautifully restored fiddle and invited me to play *Good Bye Johnny Dear*, a tune I had namechecked once too often in the preceding weeks when bragging about my progress.

I could still remember the opening notes, F, F, E, D, D, F, A, B, A, B, C — Goodbye Johnny dear/ When you're far away/ Don't forget your dear old mother/ Far across the sea — and stumbled through them before screeching to a painful halt and having to confess to my shocked parents that I had fiddled the fiddle money to spend at the picture houses.

'The proof of the pudding is certainly in the eating,' was my mother's sad comment. She was bitterly disappointed — and yet she would never again bring up the subject of my musical truancy.

I walked down to the spring well in John Hunt's field — the village water supply and informal social focus since long before the introduction of indoor taps — went down on my knees and, plunging my head into the water, drank the clear, cold elixir while offering a prayer of sorrow and repentance for my four wasted years. I then stood up, took several deep breaths, and headed for the house.

As I approached the old place I was shocked to see that the little front garden, long my parents' pride and joy, was no more. Since my last visit, Mayo County Council had widened the Galway road, and not only our garden but also the little hedge-lined pathway to the house had been a casualty.

Our house was now below road level and had steps down to the front door. The bigger garden to the right had survived, but I could only imagine how traumatic the change must have been for my parents.

I swallowed hard, tapped on the door and pushed it open with a casual and cheery greeting: 'What's happening?'

I saw the shock and emotion register on my parents' faces. My mother ran to me, tears streaming, and hugged me furiously. My father seemed frozen in his low chair, paralysed with a mixture of surprise and anxiety.

'Thank God, thank God, you're home!' my mother kept saying. 'Why did you not let us know when you were coming? We'd have had the place a lot more tidy.'

'I would not worry at all about that,' I assured her. 'I'm just glad to see you both. Is there a drink at all in the house? There's nothing I'd like better now than a bottle of stout.'

'We'll have the tea first,' my mother said quietly. 'You'll have plenty of time for stout.'

It seemed she already suspected I was developing an unhealthy fondness for the demon alcohol as a way of easing pain and coping with depression.

We sat for a long time by the open hearth — watching the turf fire burn and talking about everything except my time in Tennessee. They were clearly thrilled to have me home, but I could also see my father was not coping well with retirement. He was unsteady on his feet and emotional, and I thought how hugely difficult must have been the past few years for my mother as she watched his decline.

'Tell me,' my mother said after we had skirted the issue for about three hours, 'how did the big day of your graduation go?'

'I'll tell you all about that in the morning,' I said with forced nonchalance, rising from the hearth. 'I'm just going for a short walk into town, just to clear the head, and we'll have a good chat over breakfast. Don't wait up for me — I have a few people to call on.'

It was getting late, but I knew the one bottle of stout my mother had proffered would not be enough to satisfy my thirst on this day and night of homecoming. And so I set off toward Ballyhaunis and the lights of Mick Morris's Horseshoe Inn, my hometown equivalent of Sammy's Apex in Johnson City, Tennessee.

35

Barstool Hero

I WAS soon perched on a high stool in the Horseshoe Inn in Abbey Street, about 50 yards from the Railway Bridge on the edge of town, and Mick Morris welcomed me home with a first pint on the house.

The cool, dark Guinness tasted bittersweet, because my mind was still in turmoil and in my heart I knew I should still be sitting by the fire keeping my ageing parents company. Such thoughts were nagging when my father's brother Paddy joined me at the bar.

Uncle Paddy was quite a character and we always got on well. There were times he would arrive in the Horseshoe and drink alone, totally ignoring me and his many friends. When he was in form though, there was no better company; he would spin great tales about growing up in Drimbane and later working at a variety of jobs in London — or as he called it, the British capital.

He offered his customary greeting: 'How are you, my friend?'

I assured him on this night of my homecoming that I was extremely well and he allowed me to buy him his first drink of the night. Soon we were exchanging lively stories, myself recounting hair-raising experiences from the Appalachians, Paddy countering with colourful adventures of his own.

Before long we had an audience of fellow drinkers and talkers, several telling me I was still a sporting hero in Ballyhaunis and would long reap the benefits of that status. I felt increasingly like a fraud but dared not puncture their enthusiasm. And I refused none of the complimentary pints being set up in quick succession on the counter in front of me.

My father had two brothers, Jack and Paddy, and I was very fond of both of them. Sitting on the high stool that night I had flashbacks of lovely innocent days working with Uncle Jack at big Fair Days in Ballyhaunis. I was only a slip of a lad when I went taking what was known as 'custom' in 'The Gap' at the top end of town.

The Fair Green, where cattle were bought and sold once a month, was owned by a local merchant, Jack Dillon, and had two entrances: a very wide one opposite the Parish Church and a small one, 'The Gap', between the Parochial House and Tighe's the Cobblers down the street.

When an animal was sold on the Fair Green, the buyer put his mark in red or green raddle on its back. That also meant the payment of custom when the animal exited the Fair, which was how Jack Dillon secured revenue for the lease of this fine space.

Uncle Jack took custom at the big exit and proved himself tenacious and resourceful when dealing with rough jobbers as they wheedled or bullied or stormed the exit in a bid to dodge payment. Armed with a stout ash plant, Jack would stand his ground in the breach and enforce the law.

Small and skinny as I was, I too held my ground down at the smaller gap. Again wielding a strong ash plant, and shouting loud and often — 'Custom! Pay your custom! No custom, no exit!' — I earned a reputation for fearlessness in the face of jobbers trying to hustle and rustle cattle through The Gap and across the street to Annie Freely's holding yard.

Despite laying down the law, I got on well with the dealers and ended up working for several — the Webbs, Tighes, Morans and Cruises, to mention just four. They were colourful characters, and even then I was drawn toward people who danced to a different rhythm.

I did a lot of droving, taking cattle on the hoof from fair to farm, and loved hanging out with the dealers. There were even times when I considered jobbing as a career path — especially when I overheard Sean Tighe tell his fellow dealer Francie Cruise, 'That young Greally, he's only a lad but he's a good judge of a beast.' I was 14 but I felt ten feet tall that day.

Such thoughts ran through my head as I stood before the mirror in the toilet of the Horseshoe near closing time. Uncle Paddy had gone home an hour earlier, leaving me to work my way through a rake of free pints, and I was dog tired and unsteady on the feet.

For a long time I gazed at the face in the mirror and tried to figure out how my American dream turned so sour after I had gone west full of promise and expectation. I returned to my perch at the bar to finish off the last pint.

'The parents must be delighted to have you back,' Mick Morris said. 'Are you home for good or have you more college time to finish up?'

'I think I'm finished in more ways than one,' I replied, and Mick laughed heartily with me at that rueful joke.

I wandered back under the railway bridge and up through lower Devlis, humming *These Are My Mountains*, a song I had last sung in the famous Carter Family Store in Hiltons, Virginia.

For fame and for fortune, I've wandered the earth,
And now I've returned to the land of my birth;
I've brought back my treasures, but only to find,
They're less than the pleasures I first left behind.

Tears flowed down my cheeks as I sang that first verse. I recalled giving the song full blast on the stage in Virginia with our little ballad group, The Irish Rebels, and how that same night my great friend Ray McBride had danced wild jigs and held the place in thrall.

Now the party was over and my long-suffering mother would soon be reminding me 'the proof of the pudding is in the eating'. I was not at all looking forward to the morning and our conversation over breakfast, but I kept on singing as I staggered toward home.

36

A Mother's Love

NEARING the house I searched through pockets and was relieved to confirm I had brought the front-door key; it was well past midnight and my parents would surely be in bed — and having to break the bad news about my non-graduation could wait at least another few hours.

I noticed a light in the kitchen window but reckoned my mother had left it on so I would make as little noise as possible on my return. And so I was surprised on entering the kitchen to see she was still up, sitting by the fire, directly under a large framed photo of me taken at the 1971 *Western People* Awards.

I would have preferred if that photo had been given less prominence, but it had long held pride of place for my mother. And on this night, as I staggered into the kitchen, I felt deeply ashamed seeing her sitting there under it and looking sadly into the embers still glowing in the grate.

'You took your time,' she said quietly but with emphasis on the final word.

'I thought you'd be long gone to bed,' I replied. 'I met a lot of people and uncle Paddy as well, so the night really flew.'

'You'd better eat something before you go to bed,' she said, walking to the table and uncovering a plate of ham sandwiches.

As I wolfed down the sandwiches along with several cups of tea, she studied me intently and said, 'What's happened you at all? You look the worse for wear and you couldn't even settle for a few hours since you arrived home.'

'I'm fine,' I assured her. 'I just need a few days to adjust to being home, and it's not as if I intend to be rushing off back to Tennessee. I'll be around for a good while now and we'll have lots of time to catch up on everything.'

'You didn't finish your time in college?' she said, more in statement than by way of a question.

'It's a long story, but you're right — I went off track a bit this last year,' I said.

Her response came as a huge relief: 'The main thing is you're home safe now and I prayed to God every night that you would be all right. We'll say no more about Tennessee. All that matters is that you're back with us. It has not been easy here this long while, especially with your father's depression getting worse all the time.'

It occurred to me to tell her I too had been afflicted with bouts of depression, but I knew she already had more than enough on her plate.

'It should make a big difference now to your father that you're home,' she continued. 'He missed you terribly, and you know that I did too.'

Another wave of guilt washed over me as I sat there in silence watching the dying embers. I felt a bit tipsy and light-headed but also profoundly sad.

I listened as my mother talked of how father had struggled since retiring from work on the Friary Farm: 'He started to go downhill the day he finished. He could not wait to hit 65 and retire and it was the worst thing he could have done. There are days now when he doesn't get up at all.'

My mother had usually been the strong one who kept things together on the home front. She had always looked on the bright side, even in the bleakest of times, and it was surely her constant thought of others that kept her going. She had cared for her father for many years, all the way until his passing in his early 90s, and among neighbours and friends she had earned a reputation for integrity, discretion, kindness and good cheer.

The only time I had seen her falter was when her dear sister, Eileen, died suddenly. She went to pieces for a long while after that, but she showed her resilience by bouncing back in time to attend Tom's ordination in Rome.

She was, like so many Irish mothers of the time, fiercely proud of having a son a priest, and I always felt that visit to Rome was her happiest moment. Of course we should have gone as a family, but money was tight and my parents could afford only the one plane ticket.

Sitting by the hearth in Devlis, I brooded on how I had again let her down. I recalled the evening she proudly presented me with the restored fiddle only to learn I had been dodging lessons. There was the day I arrived home with my Inter Cert results — three honours but a failure in maths that meant there would be no certificate.

On those occasions I saw in her eyes a disappointment that pierced me to the heart. She had the same look now as I got ready to head for bed.

'I won't call you too early,' she said quietly.

'I think that's a good idea,' I replied as I climbed the stairs.

The old bedroom was warm and welcoming, the bed lovingly made up and a hot-water bottle nestling between fresh, crisp sheets — clearly my mother had gone to great trouble to make sure everything was perfect for me.

I undressed, went down on my knees and said a prayer for my parents and an act of contrition for myself, and got into bed.

Across the landing, my father was snoring soundly. I heard my mother's footsteps advancing up the stairs. And when she called out softly, 'Good night,' I stifled the sobs so she would not hear my distress.

It was a long time before sleep arrived. My mind went back to early mornings during my childhood and the noising of cattle being driven on the hoof to Ballyhaunis Fair.

Thomas Wolfe wrote of the haunting and lonesome sound of

the whistle and the tolling of the bell as freight trains rolled across the vast American continent. For me the most evocative sound had always been the bawling of those cattle and the shouts of the drovers in the dark hours before dawn.

My father used to worry on those fair days that some feisty animal would jump the low fence into our garden. And on the rare occasions when it happened he would survey the trampled seed rows or the damage to his prized potato ridges and be almost inconsolable.

I thought too about early mornings when Pat Cribbin would arrive outside our house and his low whistle would signal time to pull on the running gear and head off 'around the road'.

Thinking about lost innocence, and how in Tennessee running had become more a chore than a joy, and of my mother's sadness — and wondering confusedly where I might go from here — I eventually drifted off to sleep.

37

Turning The Page

IT was near midday when I surfaced to greet my first full day home in Devlis. I lay for a while gazing at the ceiling, trying to gather my thoughts and scramble what I could remember from the night before. I was back where I had started out from and I wondered what lay ahead for me.

As usual when I got anxious, I started to hum a tune, and this time it was a comforting little song called *Home*:

'The miles that lay behind weren't as hard as the miles that lay ahead/ And it's too late to listen to the words of wisdom that my daddy said/ And the straight and narrow path he showed me turned into a thousand winding roads/ My footsteps carry me away, but in my mind I'm always going home...'

I could hear my parents talking downstairs but could not make out what they were saying. I was sure, however, that I was part of the conversation, and the prospect of going down to face them increased my anxiety. What came back to me then were childhood mornings when I would lie in bed hearing the busy chatter of women downstairs talking to my mother over cups of tea. These were what I called the Women of the Well — half a dozen near neighbours who regularly dropped into our house on their way to or from the well with buckets of spring water.

I dreaded those Saturday mornings when I itched to get to the newsagents in Ballyhaunis for the *Dandy*, *Victor* and *Hotspur*, comics for which I had a standing order. I was too shy to go downstairs while the women chatted and I counted the minutes until the voices faded and I knew the last of them had left.

We had no piped water in Devlis in the early fifties — or for that matter electricity; the Aladdin lamp and the Tilley lamp, both fuelled by paraffin, were our main sources of light.

The drawing of water from the well was a daily ritual. The women would pass by our house in pairs, usually calling to my mother as they passed: 'Were you above?'

When the question came from a woman passing unaccompanied, my mother would invariably reach for her scarf and an empty bucket and go out.

Even at a young age I discerned that my mother was a valued confidant for those Women of the Well, and when one of them arrived at our gate alone it was likely to mean some important matter needed to be aired. In this close-knit but oddly competitive community differences would arise, and usually it fell to my mother to broker the peace.

I continued with my musings until I remembered something my grandfather Harry Mannion had told me: 'If you're ever lying in the bed thinking about getting up, you have to just push the bedclothes up and hit the Devil in the face. The Devil wants you to be slothful and idle and you must not fall into that trap.'

It was advice I never forgot, even during my darker days in Tennessee. And so I hopped out of bed, had a quick wash and shave, and headed downstairs.

Both my parents seemed in good spirits and soon I was tucking into a hearty fry and chatting to them as if I had never been away.

We covered a wide range of topics: the weather, the government, the job scene, the neighbours and near relations, the trauma of the road-widening and associated damage to the front garden.

I did not even have to skirt around the subject of Tennessee and my failure to graduate. It was as if my mother had decided that chapter was closed and the topic was off limits, and until the day they died neither of my parents ever berated me for squandering those rare educational and sporting opportunities.

The subject of Tennessee was never broached, and while that

was in one sense a relief, it also recalled for me the unnatural silence that followed the death in infancy of my little brother Gerard. It was as if my failure was too painful for my parents to discuss, or maybe they thought it would be too distressing for me to try articulating what had gone wrong.

I felt comfortable being home, but I was already missing some of my close friends back in Tennessee, especially my great friend and teacher David McClellan.

'You'll hardly go near the town today,' my mother said, and I knew what she really meant was that I could do with a break from the Horseshoe Inn and other such watering holes.

'No, I'll hang in here for today and we can do a bit of catching up,' I replied.

Seeing the relief that registered on the faces of both my parents, I poured three more mugs of tea and sat quietly by the fire with them.

38

Strained Relations

NEEDING to clear the head, I went for a ramble that afternoon over John Hunt's Hill, across the road from our house. From the top I could see the village of Lecarrow and some of the circuit where all those years ago big Pat Cribbin had introduced me to road running.

I recalled the morning in Tennessee when a letter from home brought word of Pat's fatal road accident in England and how the news had hit me like a hammer blow.

Pat and myself had been like brothers. I remembered the fun we had in those early days of running 'around the road' and I remembered too an evening when on approaching Pat's house in Lecarrow I heard coming from the shed the sound of regular, heavy thumps.

On entering the shed I found Pat stripped to the waist, gloved up, and muttering fiercely as he landed blow after blow on a sand-filled canvas punchbag hung with a sturdy rope from the rafters.

'You're in good form,' I said.

Pat came to an abrupt stop and, dripping sweat, offered his usual greeting: 'Flaming hell!'

'Flaming hell what?' I enquired, as per usual formula.

'Flaming hell! The old fella gave Brute away this morning and I'm mad as hell about that.'

Brute was the half-hound Pat and myself sometimes took hunting and Pat adored the animal.

'I've been beating the daylights out of this bag for the last half-hour because it's the only way I can contain myself,' he said.

Standing atop the hill, I wished my old pal were still around so we could again go rambling the hills, flushing hares and rabbits and dreaming big dreams. And I recalled again something else about my companion of the road that evoked a smile and a tear. It was the memory of Pat arriving home for Christmas after his first six months in England.

He came complete with a pronounced 'Brummie' accent and extremely loud clothes that seemed totally out of character. Sporting a cravat and a garish jacket and trousers, he was mad to go dancing, and the rough innocence that had set him apart was little in evidence.

It was an astonishing transformation in just a few months but it seemed life under the bright lights of Birmingham had brought out another side of my great friend.

I walked down the hill, crossed the road and headed toward the river and the more distant villages of Church Park and Drimbane. This was the territory I often tramped with my father in Novembers past, the start of the pheasant-shooting season.

The first of November was 'our day'. We would go to 6.30 Mass in the Nun's Convent, the better to get an early start on the mission my father referred to as 'fowling'.

Our dog was unusual for a Welsh corgi in that he was well capable of flushing out pheasants from the undergrowth. Given the need to cover every inch of ground the pheasant had traversed en route to its hiding place, little Roddy had to work much harder than your regular gun-dog, such as a cocker spaniel, but he had exceptional talent and never let us down.

On those November mornings we would walk for miles across fields and hills, and it was then I felt closest to my father, who except when he had a few glasses of Guinness on board, was something of a closed book.

When I was about six he would bring me into Peter Hannon's bar after last Mass on Sunday and treat me to a small glass of Guinness — a pony of stout. I would sit there proud as punch on the high stool listening to my father engage with a group of friends that often included his brothers, Jack and Paddy.

My father always referred to his older brother as 'Our Jack' and if the three brothers — Tom, Jack and Paddy — failed for any reason to meet up for a Christmas Eve drink, it was as if the season had been ruined for each of them.

There was great banter in Hannon's on those Sunday mornings. The drivers of the big steam engines would arrive in while their machines were being refuelled and rewatered up at the railway station. They always seemed to me big men with hearty laughs and strong faces charred with coal and grease.

I loved being in the company of all those grown-ups and I usually came home with a pocketful of pennies — gifts from those friends of my father.

We would arrive home well after two o'clock, which would trigger an argument between my father and mother because we had delayed Sunday dinner. The argument was always there but nothing ever seemed to change.

As with all arguments between my parents, the hard words would be followed by a strained, mutual silence that could go unbroken for days. I dreaded those long silences, and I was always delighted when a neighbour or relative arrived unannounced to break the impasse, because after the visitors left, my mother and father would resume conversation as if nothing had happened.

Those thoughts were swirling around in my head as I headed across Coen's Bog toward Uncle Jack's house in Drimbane. I thought about how little I really knew about my father and how little he had let me know about him up to now.

I knew he had worked in England during the war years and was still in England when my mother and brother moved from Drimbane to the rented house in Devlis on the first of March 1949.

I knew that date because it was written in a prayer inscribed under a picture of the Sacred Heart hanging over the fireplace —

a prayer that was always said when we knelt down each night for the family Rosary.

I knew too of my father's proud reputation as a master plasterer and how he had to find work on the land when the building trade slumped.

My father always appeared to me a man disappointed with life. He never made the bold move to purchase the house we rented in Devlis, and though a gifted tradesman, he was slow to make improvements to it.

'It's not ours,' he would say when I pressed him on the subject of renovation — though he did eventually add an indoor toilet, much to the delight of my mother.

I think my parents always hoped they would end up living in my mother's home place, but that was not what fate had ordained for them. They had a hard life, and the loss of two children in infancy, my sister and brother, took a heavy toll.

Soon I saw the smoke rising from my father's old homestead in Drimbane. I was sure Uncle Jack and his family would be pleased to see me.

39

Knocking On Doors

I ALWAYS loved visiting the village of Drimbane, especially Uncle Jack and Aunt Kitty and their son, John Stephen, in their home, originally a small, thatched dwelling but latterly transformed, much extended, with several mod cons and topped off with a shiny slate roof.

I never knew my grandfather Luke Greally but had heard many stories about him. It seems he was not so much a man of the land as a man of the people — he wasn't a medical doctor or even a nurse, but he devoted much of his later years to terminally ill neighbours at a time when tuberculosis was rampant in East Mayo. My father spoke frequently of how Luke would stay right to the end with neighbours dying from TB.

The C-word at that time referred as much to consumption as to cancer, and it was widely believed that if you stayed in the sick room till the dying person's last breath you would catch the dread disease. And so when the end was near, all the family would leave the patient.

My father told of one such instance when the family, a large one, hurried from the bedroom as the boy was about to expire. All except the youngest boy, who remained by his brother's side — only to hear the dire warning shouted through the window by an older sibling: 'Come out or you'll be next!'

There were tough times back then, and Luke Greally was in demand whenever someone was struck down by TB.

Such was his aura, the story went around that he had predicted the timing of his own death — it would coincide with the ringing of the Angelus. And sure enough, after a short illness he breathed his last at the precise moment his family heard the Augustinian Friary bell peal out six o'clock.

Uncle Jack extended the usual greeting when I walked into his kitchen: 'Christ, is it yourself? When did you arrive home?'

My uncle had many stock sayings. He would preface even mundane statements of fact with his favourite: 'On my solemn oath.' Of course you were hardly going to disbelieve a man who spoke with such conviction.

Aunt Kitty soon had the table set, and over tea and sandwiches I brought them up to date about my homecoming.

This, I believe, was the house where my father's spirit remained rooted all his life. He was a frequent visitor and, much to my mother's annoyance, was always available to help with repairs and improvements there.

'You can do everything for the Greallys above in Drimbane but nothing to improve our own place,' she would complain.

To which my father invariably replied, 'Why would I do much with it when it's not ours?'

Soon it was time to go 'rambling' again and I strolled over the bohareen to Uncle Paddy's, where Auntie Mary Anne, a force of nature who was always on the go and extremely outspoken, held court.

She too had her signature greeting: 'By jakers, Francis, you're home! Come in and tell us all about America.'

Cue another course of tea and cake and conversation with Mary Anne and Paddy, two rare and wonderful individuals — eccentric, warm and always great company.

My last port of call was Uncle Miko's, the first house as you entered the village. I found my mother's brother busy as ever, rushing around in many directions but getting very little done.

My father used to marvel how Uncle Miko could spend a full day working in the field and by evening have only half a dozen cocks of hay to show for his strenuous efforts.

Several times I saw my father arrive home of a summer evening from his own work, grab a bite to eat and, at my mother's bidding, head for Drimbane to help Miko.

'Glory be to God Almighty!' he'd exclaim as he approached Miko's place. 'Will you look at how little he has to show and him all day in the field — he might as well have been throwing stones at his jacket for all he has done.'

Father would get stuck in and within a few hours the field was all set out in neat cocks, a picture of good husbandry.

I never learned the import or provenance of 'throwing stones at his jacket' — but it sounded good and was one of my father's favourite put-downs.

A shopkeeper by training and inclination, Uncle Miko was never cut out for working the land and had reluctantly given up a good job in Ballina to take over the family smallholding only at the request of his father.

Neighbours would see him out feeding calves or struggling with routine farm chores well into the night. He was the proverbial square peg — and a deeply frustrated one at that — and it was little wonder he eventually found escape and solace in the pubs of Ballyhaunis.

Despite his domestic struggles, Miko was great company. He was widely read, and as a young lad I loved the days we spent together in the bog, he cutting and I spreading out the turf. On those days we would talk about books and writers and Gaelic football, and those common interests forged a bond between us.

On this visit I found him preoccupied, not for the first time, with farm tasks yet to be completed.

'We'll meet in town for a few drinks at the weekend,' I suggested, and he smiled a knowing smile and nodded in agreement.

I headed back across the fields toward home and found myself reciting aloud lines from one of my favourite poems: Patrick Kavanagh's *Peace*.

'Upon a headland by a whinny hedge/
A hare sits looking down a leaf-lapped furrow/
There's an old plough upside-down on a weedy ridge/
And someone is shouldering home a saddle harrow/
Out of that childhood country what fools climb/
To fight with tyrants Love and Life and Time?'

I was back home barely 24 hours but already I was restless. I would, however, give it a few months and see what unfolded during that time.

40

Bulling For Road

I HUNG out at home for several months. It felt good to be there with my parents to celebrate Christmas at the end of 1976. I had missed a few Christmases at home during my years in Tennessee and those I spent in Johnson City were painful memories.

There were four of us for Christmas dinner that year — my parents, Uncle Miko, and myself — and between us we gave the turkey a good show. My mother was at her brilliant best in the cooking department, and the turkey, done to perfection in an oven hung over the open turf fire, never tasted so good.

Even back in the bosom of my family, though, I still felt restless and ill at ease. I thought several times about returning to America but had neither the funds nor the visa to back up those fleeting fantasies. I tried to pick up the threads of my writing but with little success. I missed the interaction with kindred spirits in David McClellan's creative-writing classes back in Tennessee. In short, I was stuck in a rut and just could not seem to get my tracks in the ground back home.

A return to running at that point would surely have helped, and I was confusedly aware of that. But I felt lethargic and chronically disappointed — the one thing getting me out of bed before midday the recollection of Grandad Harry Mannion's counsel against sloth — and spent most of the time reading.

The grey mist was clinging again — more frequently and thickly than in Tennessee. Back in a depressed environment, watching my father struggle daily, I tried hard to mask my own emotional turmoil, but of course my mother was not fooled.

'Would you not go to the doctor for a bit of a check-up?' she asked.

'I'm fine — I just need to get back in the workforce again and I'll be flying.'

In truth the only place I was flying was the pub circuit in Ballyhaunis, finances permitting. I had signed on the dole and that was my one stream of income during that spell at home. When I had money, I found solace in the Horseshoe Inn and various other licensed premises, reconnecting with the resident wits, philosophers and all-round characters of the town. For my own part, I had plenty of tales to spin from my time in Tennessee.

Amid all the banter and bravado, however, John Prine kept coming back to haunt me in the form of certain song lines: *'A clown puts his make-up on upside down/ So that you will think he's smiling even when he wears a frown.'*

Kris Kristofferson was another of my favourite songsmiths, and one of his gems, *The Pilgrim*, also resonated: *'Once he had a future full of money, love and dreams/ That he spent like they were going out of style.'*

That song finishes with lines I felt had been written about me: *'He's a walking contradiction, partly truth and partly fiction/ Taking every wrong direction on his lonely way back home.'*

Many of the lyrics by my two favourite songwriters plumbed the depths of a loneliness with which I was all too familiar.

I was badly in need of a change of mood and a change of scenery, and both arrived in the form of a job that would take me on a merry jaunt all around Ireland.

Clockwise from top left: My brother, Tom, with his right hand on my shoulder and his left hand on Michael Joyce's shoulder; my parents, Kathleen and Tom Greally; back from Athenry Sports with Padraig Keane; early days with Pat Cribbin

Holy show: joining hands (first left, front row) with fellow altar boys and Fr Buckley at the Augustinian Friary, Ballyhaunis

The Mouse Greally: no prizes for spotting me, near the bottom right-hand corner, among classmates at St Patrick's College, Ballyhaunis

Dressed to kill: posing (centre of front row) as Aunt Abby with other cast members on my stage debut in Arsenic and Old Lace

Good old boys: on a visit home from Tennessee, with Uncle Miko Mannion, Uncle Paddy Greally, Uncle Jack Greally and my dad, Tom Greally

Smooth running:
Tennessee 1972
before my form
took a dive

The Irish Brigade: from left, Neil Cusack, PJ Leddy, Eddie Leddy,
Ray McBride and Kevin Breen; I'm the small one second from right

Houston no problem: NCAA 1972 heroes (back row) PJ Leddy, Neil Cusack,
Eddie Leddy and Kevin Breen; (front row) myself and Ray McBride.

Fund runners: Noel Carroll, Sean Callan, myself, Tom O'Riordan and Donal O'Riordan at a Christmas morning GOAL Mile

All for one: The Three Amigos, Matt Rudden, Harry Gorman and Sean Callan, great buddies and magnificent ambassadors for Irish athletics

Circle of friends: with Coach Walker at a reunion of ETSU alumni in Johnson City in 2010, the old differences between Coach and myself long forgotten

Rural idyll: with Ken Marion on the front porch of Wart Root Farm, an oasis in the hills where I spent many happy hours

Signature moment: Marian and myself on our great day

Seven heaven: The family on Catherine's First Communion day, (from left) Catherine, Tomás, Laura on Marian's knee, and Conor, and I'm holding Claire

Angel of mercy: Nurse Marian in working outfit

Celebrating the launching of the new magazine 'Irish Runner' were Frank Greally (centre), the editor, with former international cross-country runners Padraig Keane and Eddie Spillane.

Big news: press coverage of the launch of Irish Runner at Dublin's Oval Bar in 1981, Padraig Keane, Eddie Spillane and myself in high spirits

New baby: Checking the latest issue with Martin Joyce

Leading the way: the front cover of the first issue of Irish Runner showed Brian Keeney and Paddy Murphy shoulder to shoulder at the head of the Clonliffe 20

Full of running: Phoenix Park in the early 1980s, with the bearded Jim Dowling, wearing the black tee-shirt, in hot pursuit

Money no object: Richard and Evelyn Gallagher celebrate another issue of the magazine with Marian and myself in the mid-1980s

Wedding bells: celebrating Conor's marriage in 2014 to Tracey Wade at Inish Beg, (clockwise from above) Tom Greally, myself, Tomás and Conor; our lovely daughters Laura, Claire and Catherine; the proud parents and the cup that now cheers; two happy couples

Gratitude Run: top of page, the inspirational Hayleigh Bone leads us out at Santry; above, doing a lap of honour with Neil Cusack, Ray McBride and Ron Hill; left, no slacking with Hayleigh Bone and Thomas Branigan Greally; top of facing page, celebrating with Tomás and Conor; centre left, flying with Laura and Claire; centre right, with Tomás and Luke; bottom, mission accomplished with my coaches Catherina McKiernan and David Carrie

Thrill of a lifetime: meeting my singing and songwriting hero
Kris Kristofferson in Dublin, all thanks to my good friend Brendan Hackett

41

Stand-up Performer

IT was with some trepidation that I set out for Dublin to meet up with the driver from Lismore Coaches, the man with whom I would be working closely on my first coach tour of the country. I had talked my way into the job of tour guide, due to last the entire summer, and was already having grave reservations about my ability to deliver — especially as I had never set foot in many of the places listed on the itinerary.

Vincent Kearns turned out to be a pleasant and helpful Dubliner who soon put me at ease when I met him in the Montrose Hotel. Over a few pints that night, I levelled with him about how inadequate I was feeling, and he quickly reassured me all would be well.

'Just read up the night before on where we're going, and I'll be happy to keep you prompted as well,' he said.

The following morning we picked up our passengers at Dublin Airport — a gaggle of high-school students and their teachers from Minnesota. They were a lively bunch and it felt like I was back on a college campus again.

I adapted to my new role much more quickly than I had imagined and was soon into my stride, entertaining visitors with stories, poems and songs and everything I knew about the history and culture of the old country — and a share of stuff I didn't know.

Sometimes it was necessary to improvise, and Vincent, a great help and an excellent colleague, taught me several stratagems. If, for instance, a large and unidentified, non-flying, ruin suddenly loomed up, say on the starboard side, I would immediately turn to port and wax lyrical and at length on the richness of the arable landscape or the peculiar virtues of the resident cattle.

The diversion proved hit and miss. Often some eagle-eyed passenger would pipe up insistently from the rear, 'Mr Greally, Sir — what about that old castle we've just passed?'

And if that happened my reply was always and invariably the stock one: 'Oh, that was an O'Brien stronghold, reduced and abandoned in 1798.'

For the most part, that 14-day tour of Ireland went swimmingly; I was usually on top of my game and soon felt I had landed the dream job. And yet there were days I struggled to shake off the grey mist of listlessness and self-doubt, and my poems and stories seemed flat and uninspiring.

I was struggling in much the same way as I had done in Tennessee, and it reminded me of other grey days when I would stare for hours at a pink spot I had painted on the wall at the end of my bunk bed in Cooper Hall Dormitory. Ray McBride used to joke that I was having a 'pink spot day', and I was never able to fully share with him or anyone else what exactly was happening when the greyness descended. The only thing I knew was that when it happened what quickly followed was lethargy and an unfathomable feeling of upset that I had to fight to keep at bay.

It was bad enough in the relative privacy of a college dorm room but much worse when facing over 40 young Americans on the few mornings I really struggled.

Still, it proved largely great fun out on the road, seeing the country as I had never seen it before. This was the start of something new for me and I was already looking forward to my next tour.

The icing on the cake came on the last day of the trip, when we drove our group back to the airport. As they left the coach, each one gave Vincent and myself an envelope — our tips for the service provided.

Vincent had told me how important my stand-up performance

would be on this final day, and so with tales of famine and oppression and brave young rebels I had them practically weeping in their seats en route to Shannon Airport.

'You played a blinder there,' Vincent told me as they headed for Departures. 'You'll see just how good you were when we count the tips.'

He was on the money in every sense, and when I added up my takings I was pleasantly astonished and felt a new pep in my step and renewed hope in my heart.

That summer I traversed much of Old Ireland — learning a little more about my native land on each excursion. On the weeks when I was not touring, I headed back to Ballyhaunis or hung out with newfound friends in Tralee or Killarney. I learned how better to keep a brave face when my form dipped, but most of the time I was on a high and well capable of entertaining a coachload of Americans all through the day and many times late into the night.

By this time I had teamed up with Billy Moreland, a lively little ex-Army man from Ringsend who would be my driver for the most of that summer. Billy was a former cross-country runner and we became great friends. We also became great drinking buddies and put in many a night at the bar with some of our touring companions.

It seemed to me that on every tour of about 40 Americans, there was always a core group of no more than six who would be up for late-night sessions. The rest would be content to sip a glass of Guinness after dinner, stretch and yawn contentedly, and head for bed.

It reminded me of my first week in Tennessee. As McBride and myself set for our 6.30am run, we saw a couple of locals already coming back from their morning workout.

'Greally,' said Ray, 'I can't figure out these Americans atall — it seems to me they want to be the first to bed and the first up as well.'

The age profile of our coach groups varied, but most were of so-called 'blue rinse' vintage, well into retirement and very well heeled. It was usually the younger members who were keen to party, and if they wanted company, Billy and I were more than willing to join in the fun.

The summer passed in a blur and soon it was time to head west again. My mother and father were happy to have me back, but my feet were still itchy, and it would not be long before I took the road back east to the bright lights of Dublin.

42

No Common Bystander

IN early 1978 I replied to an advertisement in the *Irish Independent*, recruiting staff for a magazine soon to be launched in Dublin. I was keen to get back into journalism and had tried without success to get work with the provincial papers in Mayo.

The folks at home were eager for me to wait and see if a job opened up in the local post office. My father still harboured the ambition that I would one day be delivering the goods around Ballyhaunis, the hometown beat being regarded as the plum job for a postman. Although I had long since resigned from the Post Office, I think he still believed that by some miracle I would be first in line were a vacancy to arise.

My father had all his life dreamt of 'winning the Sweep' — the £50,000 jackpot in the Irish Hospitals Sweepstakes — and I think he had a better chance of that happening than of seeing me toting a mailbag again. It was a job I had enjoyed while it lasted, but I wanted more than anything to get back writing and working in journalism.

I made another trip to Dublin for the interview with Pat Ruddy, the publisher of the proposed magazine, a monthly in the 'social and personal' vein, to be called *Irish Bystander*.

I met Pat at his home in Blackrock and it turned out he too was a Mayoman, from the town of Ballina. He was already publishing the magazine *Golfer's Companion* and contributing a popular weekly golf column to the *Evening Herald*.

We hit it off, and before I left, Pat told me I could come to work for him the following week — provided I was willing to muck in and do everything from selling ads to collecting accounts and writing features. It was an all-in-one package and I grabbed the opportunity with both hands.

And so I went to work for the fledging *Irish Bystander* and joined a crew of characters every bit as colourful and diverse as those I had met on coach tours and back in Tennessee. It struck me then that I seemed to have a knack of falling in with people cast from a one-off mould, and most of the same characters were, like myself, fond of the barstool, the songs and the stories.

Fintan Cusack, advertising sales director at the *Bystander*, reminded me a lot of my old pal Benny Patrick back in Tennessee. Fintan would hold court in the bar near our office and regale us with outlandish stories of his time in Nigeria.

'There was one time when I was walked out handcuffed and barefoot across the hot sands and told I was about to be executed.' That was his introduction to a terrifying tale of how he had crossed a mafia figure in Nigeria and narrowly escaped with his life.

I could identify with many of Fintan's tall tales of close encounters and closer shaves, and of course I had many of my own Tennessee experiences to throw into the mix at those late-night sessions that became the norm for most of us working on Pat Ruddy's magazines.

Pat himself was a non-drinker and in no way a fan of the pub culture. I often wondered what he would have thought had he encountered his little band of employees on one of our livelier nights out — and there were many of those at the time.

Still, we managed to get the first issue of *Irish Bystander* afloat, and it was a fine publication that covered a variety of topics: fashion, food, hotels, property, antiques — anything and everything that might generate ad sales.

For the most part the features were paid for. It was a brilliant concept whereby the advertising team would sell a feature to a fashion house, restaurant, hotel, antique shop, whatever, and our team of writers and photographers would deliver a glowing editorial on the business in question. It meant most pages were paid for, and only about 24 pages of commissioned editorial were needed to complete the job.

Much of my work on *Irish Bystander* was in the advertising department, which soon expanded and was moved from Pat's home in Blackrock to bigger premises in Glenageary. We worked out of a basement there and every hour Pat would put his head in the door and enquire, 'Any joy?'

By 'joy' he meant of course ad sales, which he liked to track hour by hour rather than day by day. It kept us very much on our toes and it was always a relief when I was assigned to write a few features rather than staying on sales duty in a gloomy basement with little natural light coming in. It was not a great place to be on days when the form was down, but I always found some solace in the evenings when Fintan led us to the Leinsters Bar across the road.

I seldom thought of returning to running during those days at *Irish Bystander*, but then two events happened in quick succession that got me thinking again about the link I had lost with the sport since coming back home.

In 1979 I suggested to Pat Ruddy a feature on the World Cross Country Championships about to take place in Limerick. We often included a sports segment in the magazine, and Pat agreed this was something worth writing about — especially as John Treacy was defending his world title on home soil.

My old friend Ronnie Long was the PRO for the event, and I will always be grateful to him for arranging a press pass for me for that special day when Treacy led the field a muddy dance and the Irish senior men packed brilliantly to take team silver in this hugely prestigious race.

I stayed with the newlyweds — Neil Cusack and Imelda — in Limerick that weekend and it saddened me that Neil had not made the Irish team for this great event taking place in his back yard.

Like myself, Neil had been struggling to get work since returning from Tennessee, and the late seventies were lean years to be job-hunting in Ireland.

I could see the disappointment and frustration written on Neil's face that weekend. Here was a man who had coasted to victory in the US Collegiate Cross Country and the Boston Marathon and had two Olympiads in his locker — and yet he could not make the Irish team on this very special occasion.

I felt bad for him, but I knew he was resilient and would be back on top. I was proved right when within three years he won the Dublin City Marathon in a fine time of 2:13:29, and we toasted him that day in Hartigan's on Leeson Street.

It was a sodden day when John Treacy stormed to victory, driving the capacity crowd at Limerick Racecourse delirious — as well as those of us privileged to have a seat in the press box.

It was in that same press box, over several hot whiskies, that I first came to meet and chat with the sportswriting legend Con Houlihan, and I often reflect that watching John win the world title and meeting Con that same afternoon were pivotal to my next, and biggest — indeed some said craziest — career move.

I would launch a monthly athletics magazine with a heavy emphasis on distance running and the emerging boom in jogging for fitness.

43

Giant Of The Back Page

MEETING Con Houlihan that day at Limerick Racecourse was very special for me. I had become a huge fan of his Monday, Wednesday and Friday sports columns in the *Evening Press* and his fortnightly *Tributaries* in the same paper that focused on the lives of great writers and artists. I knew from reading Con that he greatly admired Thomas Wolfe as well as at least two other of my American favourites: James Agee and Sherwood Anderson.

In the months following my return home from Tennessee, about half-a-dozen citizens of Ballyhaunis, what you might describe as kindred spirits, would gather regularly outside Mike Lyons's shop in Abbey Street to discuss the affairs of the day, the nation and the world. The banter would be lively, laced with wicked wit and searching critiques of anyone careless enough to walk past.

Occasionally, one of our group would stroll into the middle of Abbey Street and look toward the railway bridge for signs of the *Evening Press* delivery van. I can still see the tall figure of Tom Gilmore, painter and decorator with a razor wit, shaking his head to signal another no-show.

When the red Anglia finally arrived in a blur and a screeching of brakes, and the young man at the wheel flung his bundle onto the pavement and roared off into the evening, and Sean Ruane, loyal farmhand at the convent and foxhunter supreme, produced the penknife and cut the twine, we would, like kids at Mike Lyons's sweet counter, grab our copies and, as one, go straight to the back page, where Con Houlihan reigned supreme.

Usually we would only skim the column before folding the paper and branching off homeward in different directions. Con's back-page column was sacred, best savoured in the comfort and privacy of home with a full pot of tea on the hob.

When we reassembled the following day around lunchtime outside Joe Regan's Corner Bar in the middle of town, Con's latest masterpiece was top of the agenda.

I was always grateful to uncle Miko for introducing me, in a manner of speaking, to Con on my return from Tennessee. I recall early-spring days on the bog, and Miko wielding the slean, lobbing in my direction the sodden sods of turf while singing praises of the great Kerryman: 'He has a way with words, a way with words, Francis. He brings you the whole game and a whole lot more. Reading his report is better than listening to the game on the wireless.'

Con's writings, in particular his *Tributaries*, got me reading voraciously again. I had devoured his delightful and hugely insightful pieces not only on Wolfe, Agee and Anderson but also on Ernest Hemingway, F Scott Fitzgerald, Walt Whitman and Henry David Thoreau, among others — the stellar figures to whom I had been introduced by David McClellan in East Tennessee.

Con's wonderfully crafted essays on artists — including Paul Cezanne, Vincent Van Gogh, LS Lowry and indeed Derek Hill — were also a joy and greatly broadened my own cultural horizons.

Before setting off by coach around Ireland that year of 1977 I had also resumed contact with John Millington Synge, Sean O'Casey and Charles Kickham, heroes of my youth. And Con got me reading again the poetry of Patrick Kavanagh, Francis Ledwidge and Dylan Thomas and opened a window for me into the world of Thomas Hardy and DH Lawrence.

When I came to live in Dublin and work for Pat Ruddy I felt that though I had never met him face to face I already knew Con well. If I happened to be working in the city centre, I would sometimes see the gentle giant from Castle Island walking along Burgh Quay on afternoons shortly after the *Evening Press* hit the streets, and more than once I watched and listened in awe from the wings as he held court in Mulligan's pub in Poolbeg Street.

That day of 1979 in Limerick when I talked with Con over hot whiskies was the beginning of a beautiful friendship that endured all the way to Con's sad passing in August 2012, during the London Olympics.

When I first met him, it seemed to me Con would somehow fill the void I had experienced since leaving my great mentor and friend David McClellan back in Tennessee.

The day after John Treacy stormed to victory in Limerick, Con's *Evening Press* piece — headlined 'The Magic Fox That Got Away' — perfectly captured the historic occasion.

'On and on he went until in the mist and rain he was away out in front like Tied Cottage in the first three quarters of the Gold Cup.

'And like Tied Cottage he came down — but it was only a slip at a splashy bend and in a few seconds only his muddy knees reminded one of it.

'In the last mile as the powerful Pole, Malinowski, began to make up ground, he seemed like a leading dog in a very scattered pack.

'But the magic fox never looked like being caught — his biggest danger was the tumult of small boys that went out like tugboats to meet him.'

As he would do in so many of his essays over the years, Con had captured perfectly the essence of a great occasion.

There is another passage from Con that has stayed with me forever — a small piece describing the last day he worked on the bog above Castle Island that touched something deep and primal inside me.

'I knew it was the last day; I was about to depart for a different world. It was also the last day that I worked with my father.

'At about six o'clock we raked the embers of the fire together and quenched them with what water we had left over and with what tea remained in the kettle. I was pierced with an infinite sadness.'

Those words conjured up for me bittersweet memories of leaving home for the first time and also leaving for the first time for Tennessee. I felt that Con and myself were very much kindred spirits. I suspected too, even before I met him, that though Con's experience of sadness and loneliness had not been different in kind from that of other men, it had been sharper, more intense. It may well have been the key to his brilliant insights into the often complex world of great writers.

Little did I realise that day when I first met Con in Limerick to what extent, as mentor and true friend, he would influence me in the years ahead.

I drank many a mug of tea with Con and his long-time 'friend girl', the wonderful Harriet Duffin, in what he called his arrogant abode, a modest house in Portobello.

Of course Con influenced and touched the hearts of many, including our great mutual friend Feidhlim Kelly, who in Con's final years was his faithful amanuensis, transcribing as the master dictated newspaper pieces from chair or hospital bed.

Con had a wry sense of humour and when during his final illness the matter of the ultimate parting was broached, he told young Feidhlim and myself, 'You'll get along without me — but maybe not as well.'

He never spoke a truer word, and several years on I still miss him terribly, and I know Feidhlim does too.

44

The Leap Of Faith

IT was a trip to the home of Irish motor racing that prompted me to think seriously about launching a running magazine. It was 1980 and I had been assigned by Pat Ruddy to write a feature for *Irish Bystander* on the National Road Relays, a team running event taking place at Mondello Park, Co Kildare.

I travelled there with Len Williams, who would take the pictures, and we enjoyed a great afternoon covering the event from many angles. Len professed amazement at the number of runners and race officials who knew me, and I was delighted to renew acquaintance with athletes, coaches and officials from all over the country.

'You're still very popular in athletics — I cannot believe how many people came up to talk to you today,' Len remarked as we left the venue. 'You should either get back into running again or start writing more about the sport.'

I think it was covering the World Cross Country in 1979, meeting Con Houlihan, and finally covering the National Road Relays that conspired to spur me into action on the magazine.

Following on from the Mondello experience, hardly a day passed that Len Williams and another great friend, Declan O'Donoghue, did not buttonhole me at lunchtime, both of them strongly urging me to take the leap of faith. The first Dublin Marathon had recently been a roaring success, and my friends realised I was still hugely passionate about the sport.

An old school pal, Michael Joyce, was also highly encouraging when I floated the idea of a new magazine. He reminded me how influential *Athletics Weekly* had been in our young lives back in

Ballyhaunis, and how Padraig Griffin's *Marathon* magazine had been another little bible we would never miss. I used to sell *Marathon* for Padraig Griffin, a man who ferried me to many a race in his trusty Morris Minor. Padraig was a man ahead of his time — a brilliant mentor who coached the Leddy brothers in Ballinamore. His magazine was well produced, a mine of wisdom and information, and essential reading for all lovers of athletics.

My own idea was of a magazine more on the style of Runner's World, which I loved to read in Tennessee. It focused heavily on mass participation, training and profiles, and I felt Ireland was now ripe for this type of 'democratic' publication, especially as the running boom seemed about to take off after the success of the first Dublin Marathon.

The last piece of the jigsaw fell into place when I attended a BHAA (Business Houses Athletic Association) cross-country race near Bray and met runners from various companies — CIE, Cadbury, Posts & Telegraphs, Garda, and others — competing side by side in a well organised event with a vibrant social dimension; after the running, everyone piled into the hall for tea, sandwiches and chat. These, I felt, were the very people who would be my readers were I to bring out a magazine.

Meanwhile, Eddie Spillane, who back in 1970 had picked me up at Heuston Station and found me digs in Capel Street, offered, from his modest resources, a loan to get the magazine up and running.

That offer came as we jogged up Knockmaroon Hill at the start of a training run. I did not take him up on the offer, but I never forgot his kindness. Within a decade of that Sunday morning five-miler, tragedy struck in the form of a heart attack and stroke while Eddie was at the World Championships in Japan, and he remained an invalid until his death in 1998.

Eddie spent his final years in St Mary's Hospital, visited more or less frequently by running friends, and the one who stayed most faithful to the end was Sean Callan, who dropped by weekly to take Eddie for walks and chats in the Phoenix Park.

When I think of Eddie Spillane, I think of a night when I met him as he logged a 30-mile training run for the National Marathon. He had limited natural ability but by sheer dint of application he won many an Ireland vest and was for years the driving force behind Donore Harriers.

As with most things in my life, I did very little if any planning for what I was about to embark on. I heard from reliable sources that a few others had also entertained ideas for a running magazine but market research had shown there would be insufficient readership to make such a venture profitable. My own thoughts on the matter had little to do with the bottom line — they were driven more by passion for the sport in which I still felt I had come up short.

And so with much encouragement from Len Williams, Declan O'Donoghue and Michael Joyce, I finally decided on an impulse to cobble together the first issue of a magazine I would call *Irish Runner*.

I wrote much of the copy for that first issue, and the pictures were mostly supplied by Brian Tansey, a full-time bank official and gifted part-time photographer.

That first issue was laid out by kind permission of Mrs Williams — mother of Len — in her kitchen in Blackrock, where aided and abetted by Len and Declan I finally managed to get the 32 pages ready for printing in Kilkenny.

How I secured a line of credit from the *Kilkenny People* printers for that first issue remains a mystery, but it was largely thanks to the kindness of a lovely man called Ben Little, the sales representative for the company. Ben and I would become close friends for many years until his passing in 1999.

Len Williams completed the page layouts well past midnight on the final day of deadline, and the three of us — Len, Declan and myself — were at Heuston Station dark and early that morning to dispatch the artwork to Kilkenny by Fastrack.

We then headed back to town and enjoyed a couple of celebratory drinks in the White Horse Tavern on Burgh Quay.

We were well fortified when we got to Dun Laoghaire for another day on the good ship *Irish Bystander* and it occurred to me that I had never told Pat Ruddy about my bold venture into publishing. I had managed to sell very few ads for my new, non-colour, publication, and I feared Pat might dismiss the venture as publishing lunacy.

I kept my head down for a few days at work, until the first issue of the magazine was delivered and I realised to my shock and dismay I had neglected to include a cover price for the newsagents. I made a frantic call to the distributors, asking them to somehow arrange for a 50p cover price to be stamped on every copy, and I was now even more apprehensive about Pat's reaction on being presented with the magazine.

In the meantime, I dropped a few copies — which I thought looked well — into RTÉ and the national papers. I also arranged a little launch in the Oval Bar in Abbey Street. I then waited in a state of high anxiety to see what the general reaction might be.

I was especially happy with the front-cover image by Brian Tansey, a photo of Paddy Murphy and Brian Keeney racing side by side in the Clonliffe 20. I could hardly wait to see the magazine sitting on the shelf in Easons, but I was also extremely worried about the print bill I knew would soon be coming through the door.

I still had not said anything about the magazine to Pat Ruddy when he came into the office to inform me Mike Murphy of RTÉ was on the phone, wanting to talk with me on the radio about some new magazine called *Irish Runner*.

'I'll tell you all about it after I take the call,' I told my puzzled-looking boss.

That radio interview with Mike Murphy was a brilliant launch-pad for *Irish Runner*, and I was greatly relieved when soon after it Pat clapped me on the back to say well done.

Little did he know then that I was about to leave his employment and go to the *Sunday Tribune* before throwing all my eggs into the *Irish Runner* basket.

45

Earning My Stripes

TAKE off your shoes. Take off your shoes and throw them in the bin!

I was sitting in the Cork office of Michael O'Connell of Three Stripe International, a man best known at the time as Mr Adidas in Ireland. Michael had liked the first issue of *Irish Runner* and had invited me to come and talk with him about advertising for Adidas in future issues.

To say that Michael was keen on Adidas would be like saying Usain Bolt is a half-decent sprinter. He lived and breathed the iconic German brand, and his office was wallpapered in blue with the Adidas trefoil logo reversed out in white.

Michael had welcomed me warmly and we were well into an engrossing chat about athletics and running in particular when he leaned over his desk and his tone changed abruptly.

'Take off your shoes,' he repeated, no longer smiling.

Up to the time of this peremptory command, things had gone swimmingly, and to my great delight Michael had said he liked *Irish Runner* and pledged advertising support — on one condition: 'You must go full colour and I'll guarantee you a double-page ad in every issue, and at your rate-card price.'

That promise now seemed in jeopardy and I had no idea why this turn in the conversation. That was until I looked down at my feet and the penny dropped — I was wearing Nike.

I laughed and played along, unsure what was coming next. I unlaced the offending shoes, Nike's latest model, walked across the office and dropped them in the bin.

As I walked back to his desk, Michael barked another order: 'Take off your socks — they have the bloody Nike logo too!'

I stood barefoot in Michael's office, still playing along but feeling slightly awkward.

'What size are you in running shoes?' Michael's tone was a little softer.

'I'm an eight' I replied, whereupon Michael lifted the phone to his warehouse manager.

'Bring up a couple of pairs, size eight, of our best trainers — and bring some medium-size vests and shorts and tracksuits, on the double.'

I sat down in front of him, and while we waited for the goods to arrive, Michael taught me a valuable lesson I haven't forgotten.

'Don't ever make that mistake again, Frank. I know you're new to this publishing game, but I take it as an insult if someone comes into this office to do business and wears anything other than Adidas. I'm letting you off the hook this time, but don't ever repeat the mistake with anyone else.'

I left the Three Stripe International office that day with a box full of Adidas kit — and the start of a lifelong friendship with Michael O'Connell, who for as long as he was with Three Stripe remained a faithful supporter of *Irish Runner*. He was as passionate as myself about the magazine and always hugely encouraging.

His lesson in diplomacy still resonates. I get annoyed when I see athletes who are sponsored by one equipment supplier casually appear in competition or on TV wearing the clothing or shoes of a rival company. I learned a lot in a short time that day in Cork, and the experience sharpened my business faculties for the challenging years ahead.

Not long after that Three Stripe meeting, my new employer, Hugh McLoughlin, called me into his office at the *Sunday Tribune*, where I was now employed, much as I had been at the *Bystander*, selling and writing copy for ad features.

Hugh got straight to the point: 'You can work for only one

publication, the *Sunday Tribune* or *Irish Runner*. The choice is yours, Frank, so make up your mind by morning.'

I was shocked but knew that Hugh at several sound reasons for the ultimatum, among them the fact that, preoccupied with the *Irish Runner* challenge, I was struggling at the *Tribune*.

There was also the 'Flyergate' debacle. I had printed promotional flyers, canvassing runners to take out annual subscriptions to the new magazine. I distributed these while running in the Phoenix Park and at weekend road races. But I made one disastrous mistake when adding a contact number — unwittingly, I inserted the switchboard number of the *Sunday Tribune* instead of the phone number of our flat.

It did not take long before the switchboard lady told Hugh there were lots of callers looking for Frank Greally of *Irish Runner* rather than him of the *Sunday Tribune*. And seemingly it annoyed the good woman that some callers had tried to engage her about marathon training and the like.

'You'll not survive with just the wee magazine,' Hugh told me, 'so I'd advise you to scrap the idea. We're opening an office in Cork and I'd like you to move there. It's a good opportunity, Frank, but I need your answer by Monday.'

My mind raced in many directions that evening as I made my way up to South Circular Road and the small flat that Marian and baby Tomás and I called home. Despite Hugh's offer, I was floundering in the *Sunday Tribune*, where every shift seemed to recall the day of my postal meltdown in Sherriff Street.

What would I do? How would we face pulling up stakes and heading for Cork. On the other hand, would Marian think I was losing my reason if I talked of giving up a full-time job. How would we survive? What were my options?

I stopped off at the Headline Bar and over a few pints tried to make sense of where I was and where we were going. I did not have a clue.

Not for the first time, I felt like a cork on a fast-flowing river, just bobbing along with no clear direction. It was scary but at the same time oddly exciting.

I took a deep draught of the black stuff, went to the payphone in the bar and called my old pal Michael Joyce, now a solicitor in Cork. It was a long time since as kids we pretended we were publishing magazines in the garden shed of the Joyce home in Ballyhaunis.

Michael had always been a calm sort, and he was at his laid-back best that evening as I tried to explain my dilemma while hyperventilating on the phone. When I had finished my outpouring I asked his verdict. Should I throw in my lot with the *Tribune* and move to Cork or take the massive risk of going it alone with *Irish Runner*?

'By the sound of it, Frank, I doubt you're inclined to relocate to Cork. I'd say give the magazine a go and I'll help you as best I can.'

'Is that all you have to say?' I asked.

'Arrah, yeah. Just give it a go. Give the magazine a go and get another issue out. I'm sure it will be fine. Just give it a go.'

And so I headed homeward to Marian and baby Tomás feeling somewhat lightheaded and more than a little bewildered, with Michael's words ringing in my ears: Give it a go! Give it a go!

'Dammit,' I said to myself as I passed the Player Wills Factory, just yards from our flat, 'I think Michael Joyce is right. I think I will give it a go!'

46

The Marian Apparition

MARIAN pledged me her full support when I arrived home and landed her with the news that I was about to quit my permanent job at the *Sunday Tribune* and, on the advice of my friend Michael Joyce, 'give it a go' with *Irish Runner*.

I knew that she too was scared, because we really had nothing to fall back on except some superannuation money she had received when, after the birth of Tomás, she gave up nursing in the Coombe Hospital to become a full-time mother.

I had met Marian one night in Coman's Pub, Rathgar, back in 1979 and later on that night got to dance with her at a house party in nearby Leinster Road. We left that lively party around dawn and I walked Marian back to her flat on Longwood Avenue, just off the South Circular Road, knowing I had met someone special.

It was a while though before our romance fully sparkled, but on many mornings as I waited for a bus outside my flat, I'd see her strolling toward me on her way home from a night shift in the Coombe — a sight that always gladdened my heart and got my pulse racing.

We would chat and I would ask her out, but she was always coy about making further commitment. One morning I gave her a little note with the telephone number of my flat included, and I kept on hoping she might decide to call me.

Then one evening as I was about to exit the house and hit the town with Kevin Healy, a pal from Ballyhaunis, the phone rang in the hallway. As usual, Miss Sherlock, the lovely old lady who lived downstairs, was quickest off the mark, and with her hand over the mouthpiece she turned to me with a knowing smile: 'There's a lady called Marian looking for you. Do you wish to speak to her?'

Wonderfully discreet, Miss Sherlock was always a great woman to screen my phonecalls. 'I'll take that call for sure,' I said, grabbing the handset.

Marian sounded bright and breezy at the other end of the line. She told me I had crossed her mind while she ironed her uniform, and she wondered if I still wanted to take her out.

'We're just heading out the door now and my friend Kevin and myself will pick you up,' I told her. 'We're all set for a good night on the town.'

'If I'm going out at all it will be just with you,' Marian asserted. 'I don't want anyone tagging along.'

And so I went to meet the woman who would within a couple of years become my wife, and Kevin went off to have a drink or three on his lonesome.

I had linked up with Kevin, his brother Eamonn, and two other sons of Ballyhaunis, Oliver Concannon and Kieran Folliard, when I returned to work in Dublin, and we had some rare times in a flat on Leinster Road in the days before I moved to South Circular Road to team up with a new flatmate, Derek Casey from Limerick.

We were all party animals and life was never dull in that house in Leinster Road. One night I was up to my usual habit of reading late in bed, and across the room in another bed was Oliver Concannon, who with the light going full glare was struggling to nod off. As on many another occasion well past midnight, Oliver was not shy about complaining.

'Switch off that feckin' light!' he roared as I turned another page and assured him, 'One more chapter, Oliver, and I'll be finished for the night.'

On hearing that response for the umpteenth time, Oliver snapped, reached under the bed, grabbed a shoe, and with unerring aim took out the brightly burning bulb that was causing his distress. There was a loud explosion and the sound of tinkling glass as the room plunged into darkness.

'That'll teach you,' said Oliver in triumph. 'Goodnight now and don't bother your arse buying a new bulb.'

That first date with Marian went like a dream. We got on brilliantly and talked for hours over drinks in a pub on Harold's Cross Road. It was the start of our relationship, and before long we were often joined on nights out by Kevin Healy and his new girlfriend, Mary Fitzgerald, who by coincidence worked with Marian in the Coombe.

The four of us had some rare times together, especially on weekend trips in Kevin's trusty motor to Achill. Sadly, Mary, who later married Kevin, is no longer with us, plucked away far too soon by illness some years back. Kevin's brother Eamonn, another great friend, was also called home much too young,

One night in Achill we returned from the pub to find our tent blown clean across the campsite. In the gale and driving rain it was out of the question to salvage the situation, and so in the dark of night we went looking for bed and board.

We struck gold at first port of call when the woman of the house — after looking us up and down and interrogating us for several minutes — eventually relented and offered us one room with four beds.

When we got ourselves modestly settled and turned out the light, all we could see on various perches around the room were glowing statues, half a dozen or more, ranging from various saints to the Blessed Virgin to Our Lord himself. It was enough to ensure we all stayed very pure that night — knowing that into the bargain we would have to face our stern hostess in the morning for breakfast.

I got on well from the start with Marian's parents, Tom and Molly, as well as her brothers and sisters when I got to visit the Fitzpatricks in Ballingarry, Co Tipperary. I loved the weekends spent there, and the Saturday night singing sessions in a little pub known as Jackie Walsh's at the crossroads a couple of miles outside the village and close to the Fitzpatrick homestead.

Marian made a big impression too when I introduced her to my own parents, and I could see my mother was more than a little surprised and happy to see me in a relationship with someone to whom she took an immediate liking.

When after several months of going out I announced to colleagues at the *Irish Bystander* that Marian and myself were thinking of getting wed, my old pal Fintan Cusack, fortified by several large whiskies, sprang into action.

'Let me organise everything for you, Frank,' insisted my larger-than-life friend. Of course I laughed as Fintan held court in the bar of the Leinsters Pub in Glenageary, but a few days later when he bounded into the office I realised to my astonishment that he was deadly serious.

'Okay, Frank, I have two dates in June for you to choose from. I have the church in Ballybrack, close to where I live, arranged and I've wangled a special deal with the Dalkey Island Hotel for the reception that will cost you very little. I've offered them generous promotion in the *Bystander*, compliments of Pat Ruddy, who by the way is delighted to hear you've decided to tie the knot.

'I have a deal done as well to get you a suit from Magee of Donegal, so you have no excuse. Just decide the date you want to march her down the aisle.'

And so Marian and I got married in a fever and, true to his word, the bold Fintan arranged much of that very special day for us.

Most of Marian's family were there. Mother and uncle Miko came up from Mayo. Neil Cusack and Ray McBride were there too, as well as a host of friends from both sides.

The only notable absentees were my father, who was in hospital in Mayo, and my brother, Tom, who was far away in Australia. I would have given a lot to have them both there on that day of days.

Marian was stunningly beautiful on a day of sunshine and good cheer, and we celebrated our great day in style with family and friends.

The next morning we headed for a music session in Slattery's of Capel Street and I arranged a lift for us afterwards to Galway, where we spent the night before boarding the boat for a week on the Aran Islands, which was about as much as we could afford.

I often think back, though, on how feckless and unfair I was to suggest spending our first day as a married couple at a midday music session, followed by a hitched ride to Galway. It was typical of the whirlwind and topsy-turvy way I lived back then — never thinking, just careering forward with three wheels on the wagon.

After an idyllic week on Aran, it was back to 302 South Circular Road and frugal but happy living in a two-bedroom flat. Tomás was our firstborn of five children, and he was five before we managed to jump clear of flatland and purchase a house on New Ireland Road, Rialto — by which time our first daughter, Catherine, had arrived and *Irish Runner* had made a big impact on the running scene.

Marian played a leading role in those early years of the magazine, doing a brilliant job to ensure an ever-growing subscription base was kept updated, as well as addressing and wrapping the hundreds of magazines that needed to be dispatched when each issue was printed. She was a tower of strength, contending too with the many occasions when my mood plummeted and the grey mist descended.

I also have the people who took out subscriptions to thank for keeping the magazine afloat through those early years. But for their support we would have gone under in the first year of publication, especially when at year's end I decided to publish the full results of the Dublin City Marathon in a 'bumper edition' that attracted far too few paid advertisements.

I was publishing with my heart rather than my head, but between newsagents' sales and subscriptions we somehow managed to stay afloat. I still remember running through the

Phoenix Park at that fraught time carrying a bundle of subscription leaflets that I liberally distributed to any runners and would-be runners I met.

It was an especially tough time for Marian, since my organisational skills were scattered at the best of times and I was much more focused on a romantic vision than financial reality.

Ultimately, it was reader loyalty that keep our little ship from sinking, and that continues to be the case to this day. It told me I was 'doing something right' even if I was doing it in my own highly erratic way — there was madness in my method that could be woefully frustrating and stressful for those trying to work closely with me.

It was only in 1985 when Martin Joyce, a brother of Michael's, came on board as advertising and marketing executive that we began to find calm water for *Irish Runner* — and the hope as well of getting a house for our growing family.

I wonder too how or where we would have ended up had I not had the great good fortune to meet Sean Callan, the man whom I always credit with putting a permanent roof over our heads.

Sean is a true athletics aficionado and is also streetwise in the best sense. It was he suggested to me that it was time to get out of flatland and get a proper home for my family, and it was he came up with the plan that resulted in us getting a mortgage.

Sean, who has always been very much a man of the world, was in no way fazed when I told him I had zero savings.

'I'm living on the interest of what I owe,' was my black joke whenever he suggested I go house-hunting.

'Frankie,' he would say (addressing me as he always did), 'I know a man who has great connections with a building society, and he knows a man in the society who might look favourably on giving you a loan, especially if I vouch for you.'

I had hardly two coppers to rub together, but something wonderful happened when I followed Sean's advice and with much trepidation and little faith applied to the First National

Building Society. Not long after, to my utter astonishment, I was approved for a mortgage — a real miracle moment for us as a family.

Then it was time to look for the house, and there was no better man to find a 'des res' than the bold Sean, who not only identified the property on New Ireland Road but also negotiated with the auctioneer and secured a brilliant deal way below the original asking price.

We moved in January 1985 and by May we were a family of five: Marian, myself, Tomás, Catherine and Conor. We felt a little more secure at last and the magazine was making strides.

47

Long-distance Runner

THE loyal support of readers and advertisers was what kept
Irish Runner afloat in the early years after launching, and I can only
smile now when I flick through bound copies from those years and
wonder how many of our readers had a clue of the high-wire act
the editor was engaged in.

The good ship often sailed in choppy waters, none more choppy
than when Marian and I struggled to make ends meet in a little flat
beside the Player Wills factory on South Circular Road. Marian's
brother Tom and his wife, Lorrie, and kids would often be roped
in to wrap and address magazines for postal subscribers.

It was tough going — my old boss Pat Ruddy was almost
proven right when he predicted that a specialist sports magazine
would not survive in the Irish market — but we soldiered on and
I am proud to say we never skimped on quality.

I always wanted to bring readers good writing and good
photographs and I believe that is why to this day *Irish Runner* enjoys
the loyalty and support of readers and advertisers.

I was lucky from the start to have a good team around me —
Len Williams and Declan O'Donoghue, who helped cobble together
the first few issues, and Brian Tansey, bank official and athletics
aficionado as well as brilliant photographer who shot many of the
covers.

Jim Dowling was an early contributor, and I have lovely
memories of dropping by his home in Phibsboro to collect copy.
The door was always open and Big Jim inside clattering away on
his portable typewriter while Tammy Wynette or Dolly Parton
blasted from the stereo in the kitchen.

Jim was a true pioneer who encouraged me to give plenty of space to women's athletics, his specialist subject. Sadly, he died well before his time.

Dave Dempsey, Noel Carroll, Lindie Naughton, Tom O'Riordan, Mary Butler, Louise McGrillen, PJ Browne, Gerard Hartmann, Brendan Hackett, Noel Henry, Dick Hooper, Pat McCourt, Brendan O'Shea, Liam Moggan, Mick McKeon, Sean McGoldrick and James O'Brien supplied a great mix of written content.

Stephen Humphreys started his photography career with us and went on to become a full-time, award-winning professional with the *Irish Independent*. He always reminds me that it was *Irish Runner* set him on his way.

Arthur Boland was another of our photographers, a runner himself who built a great image archive of the contemporary athletics scene.

Jim Dunleavy from Ballina sold ads for us, and for good measure was great company.

Whenever I needed a sounding board during those early years, I looked no further than Noel Carroll, a man I still think of with every passing day. Noel was one of my heroes and I cherish memories of watching him and Frank Murphy completing their daily training sessions in College Park during the early 1970s, when I first arrived to work in Dublin.

Noel always found time to encourage aspiring athletes like myself and when I brought out *Irish Runner* he was there as mentor and friend. The qualities I admired most about Noel were his integrity and total loyalty. He was never afraid to speak his mind but he cared deeply for his friends and helped me — and, I know, a good many others — over personal crises.

I still see Noel sitting on a stool in City Hall tucking into his lunch of banana sandwiches on brown bread and holding forth on athletics, literature and the state of the world.

He was a fount of wise and pithy sayings. My favourite: 'There is no such thing as bad weather — only weak men.'

Noel was the original marathon guru and without his influence with the City fathers and the Garda there would hardly have been a Dublin Marathon. He was a guiding light for me at many stages of *Irish Runner* and his spirit still shines.

I was blessed to discover the Sportsfile agency in the mid-1980s, and since then Ray McManus and his team have delivered brilliant images. My son Tomás has developed into a top-class photographer, often working for Sportsfile.

I'm glad to say that all our children — Tomás, Catherine, Conor, Laura and Claire — served their time at ground level on *Irish Runner*, distributing promotional flyers and selling copies of the magazine at events all over Ireland while learning early that publishing, like so many endeavours, is a team effort requiring all hands on deck.

They all ran too and got a taste of competition in what used to be the Minathon, a kids' event that took place in conjunction with the Dublin City Marathon. And Conor has twice run the full Dublin Marathon.

The years between 1984 and 1988 will always stand out for me, as it was during those halcyon days that we had on board two hugely talented and colourful individuals.

Peadar Staunton was our graphic designer during that purple patch of publishing and Richard Gallagher was our motor-cycle courier, chief sub-editor, writer and occasional illustrator all rolled into one. Together, with the help of Martin Joyce in Sales and Marketing and the all-important Accounts, we made a lively team.

Peadar, another son of Mayo, arrived just out of art college in 1984, carrying an airbrush illustration of a sprinter he hoped I might consider for our Olympic issue. That was the start of a great working relationship and friendship. Peadar went on to work for *Runner's World* in England before wandering back home to set up his own graphic design company in Tralee.

Richard was a milkman with Premier Dairies when he handed in a little essay describing his Dublin Marathon travails. That piece caught my eye and soon the milkman had relinquished his round and become a sub-editor and writer.

He went on to work full-time for several national newspapers and still frequently reminds me that it was I gave him his start in journalism when he was already middle-aged and facing redundancy.

Incidentally, the fact that after all these years and all our roads diverging, Peadar designed the cover for this book and Richard helped by reading the proofs and offering suggestions seems to me another lovely instance of life and relationships running full circle.

We were blessed with other excellent designers over the years, including Alec Tuohy and Derek Brown.

When Peadar Staunton moved to London, Michele Carroll, sprint champion and Olympian, did a great job before handing the baton to Mary Guinan, who carried it until Denise Campbell took over.

These days the page layouts are in the capable hands of Fergal Norris and John O'Farrell at Outburst Design.

Conor O'Hagan has been another long-time friend and contributor in all weathers and over many years, writing and editing and advising — a consummate professional. And of course I cannot forget my good friend John Walshe of Ballycotton 10 fame, who has also contributed greatly.

I have Paul Moloney of Adidas Ireland and Jim Aughney of the Dublin Marathon to thank for adding a new dimension to *Irish Runner* when the inaugural *Irish Runner* 5 Mile Road Race was launched in 2002. That event — now part of the widely popular SSE Airtricity Dublin Race Series — was conceived in Heathrow Airport as Paul, Jim and myself waited to catch a plane back to Dublin.

The inaugural Adidas *Irish Runner* 5 was an instant success. Of course Paul Moloney knew the running market well. A former scholarship athlete at Providence, Rhode Island, he was both passionate about athletics and mindful of what worked best for Adidas — and he backed two winners when sponsoring the Dublin Race Series and the Dublin Marathon.

I suspect it was Paul and another great friend, Gerard Hartmann, who conjured up the ticket for my trip to Kenya in 1999, when along with Gerard and Fr Liam Kelleher I saw up close how the Kenyans lived and trained.

We met the legendary Colm O'Connell, coach and Christian Brother, and received wonderful hospitality from the steeplechase icon Moses Kiptanui. All in all, a wonderful and unforgettable adventure at a time when my flagging spirits needed it most.

During the more difficult years when I was out on my own, Mary Coghlan helped me keep the magazine on an even keel, and I will always be grateful for her secretarial expertise and endless patience. I also received great support from Noel Kenny and another friend, Seamus McCartin, often helped keep me on track.

These days it's great to be working with a new generation of writers — great talents and friends such as Feidhlim Kelly, Cathal Dennehy, Donal Glackin and Ian O'Riordan, lively lads who in their passion and bounce remind me of my younger self of all those years ago. I'm delighted to report that the indefatigable Lindie Naughton is still on board, and the highly versatile and professional Rory Hafford is never more than a phonecall away.

It's eight years now since *Irish Runner* joined forces with Athletics Ireland and those years have been special as the magazine continues to thrive thanks to robust support from CEO John Foley and his staff at HQ in Santry.

I see there the massive amount of work that goes in at the coal-face to ensure athletics continues to flourish, and in retrospect I can marvel at the huge amount of work over many years by the volunteers and staff of BLE before athletics was put on a more professional footing.

Working for Athletics Ireland has been deeply fulfilling, and I like to think I have brought a few things to the table as well — the

Remembrance Run 5k and other initiatives I hope will leave a lasting legacy.

Irish Runner magazine has given me a whole lot over 34 years, and when I think back I sometimes have to pinch myself to be sure I'm not dreaming. In my wildest imaginings, I never envisaged all of this good fortune to have come my way — especially on that morning when at Heuston Station we put the artwork for the first issue on Fastrack for the printers in Kilkenny.

I can only hope that *Irish Runner* and now www.irishrunner.com are both here for the long run. The magazine has opened many doors for me and those dear to me, and I have much to be grateful for.

48

Friend In Need

I WAS going through what my friend Pat Falvey termed 'a rough patch' as I approached my 45th birthday. Several parts of my life, at home and in business, had come crashing around me. I had moved out of the house, and a long-time business partnership I foolishly thought was on solid ground had split apart.

It was during this traumatic time that I climbed Carrauntoohil on three occasions with Falvey, mountaineer, adventurer and motivational speaker. I believe those three ascents of the great mountain, in the grip of winter, significantly helped me weather my personal storms.

On the third ascent, about halfway up Curved Gully, Pat asked me how old I was. The question caught me by surprise. Why had he asked? Did he think I was fit for my age? Did he think I looked older or younger than my 45 years? Was he comparing me to the athlete he knew I once had been?

I gave him the true figure but had to ask why the question, and I will always remember his answer.

'I was thinking you were somewhere around that mark,' he said. 'You know there are only 15 years left until you hit 60.'

Of course I laughed and reminded him that from where I stood on the mountain 60 was still a lifetime away.

Some 12 years on — 12 years that just seemed to have vanished — I heard Pat on the car radio talking about his Antarctic team's latest heroics. Since our days on Carrauntoohil, the intrepid Corkman had climbed, not once but twice, the highest peak on each of the seven continents, including of course Everest. He had also survived numerous other adventures and misadventures. In coming close to serious injury or death many times, Pat had truly lived and affirmed his existence.

Listening to Pat on the radio that day made me wonder just what I had been doing over those 12 years that had slipped by so fast. I had not been climbing mountains. I had walked and run, but only in fits and starts. And the big contradiction for me was that I loved to walk and I loved even more to run. It seemed to me I had for far too long been denying myself a pleasure that was once the hub of my life.

Between 45 and 50 I was reasonably fit, and in my 50th year I wrote in *Irish Runner* about golden days walking and running in the great outdoors. And then I dropped the baton, the pounds piled on again, and though preaching in the magazine about the need to exercise I failed to follow my own advice.

I was engaged too in the perennial battle with alcohol, the only medicine that was helping me keep a brave face to the world when the black dogs came barking — as they frequently did.

I was out on my own now like a high-wire artist with vertigo and no safety net, struggling desperately to keep balance, and at every wrong turn I seemed to hear my mother's words ringing in my ears: 'Can you do nothing right, Francis?'

The truth was that alcohol had stalked me ever since, in an attempt to deaden my loneliness in the big city, I had walked across Capel Street for those two bottles of Guinness that I brought back for consumption in my bedroom in the digs.

The alcohol never failed to make me feel better about myself — at least for a time. It brought an inner glow that boosted my fragile self-esteem. Otherwise, the only situations in which I felt confident were on road, cross-country or track, when I could suddenly be fearless and on fire. But that was back a long way in my life. Now, as I approached 50, I would sit on barstools trying to make sense of the meandering road that had led me to where I was.

I had tried repeatedly to shake off the demon, but over many years alcohol had cunningly and inexorably tightened its grip. My drinking habit had very much mirrored my approach to running — going full tilt for a while, stopping for breath, then another uncontrolled burst.

Behind the mask of bluster and bonhomie, I was woefully insecure, and it seems I never trusted happiness to perch very long on my shoulder. I believe that went away back to childhood, when notwithstanding days of true bliss at home, trouble and worry were always threatening.

I recall something Jimmy Reardon said to me as we chatted about John Joe Barry's autobiography, *The Ballincurry Hare*, a book I actually published.

In the book the legendary John Joe writes of the night before he left home to head for Villanova University. He had a hired car and when he drove up to the old homestead in Ballincurry he could see through the window blinds the silhouette of his father and mother. But for some unfathomable reason, he chose not to go into the house and instead went to the haggard and there in the moonlight put his arms around an old mule he used to plough with. He then started his motor and drove off toward Shannon Airport without a backward glance.

'What was it with that old mule and John Joe?' I asked Jimmy Reardon, who had soldiered with Barry for four years in Villanova and competed alongside him at the 1948 Olympics.

'I know the real story there,' Jimmy replied. 'You see, Frank, that old mule was the only thing living that John Joe ever trusted in his life. That was all, because he could never trust himself.'

In his book, Barry plumbed the depths of his loneliness and wrote with brutal honesty about the scourge of his alcoholism. I could well empathise.

When I drank, one was never enough — or two or three for that matter; it had to be the full session to satisfy my search for nirvana.

And so back in the late 1980s, concerned about the impact at home, I signed into St Patrick's for a block of treatment, and while there I learned a lot in a short time about alcoholism, a disease I was well aware had blighted the family lives of both my parents.

I will always remember a day in the hospital when Marian and the kids visited and from the gate I watched them walk together back up the hill toward James's Street — a mother and her five young children. I vowed to myself there and then that no matter what I would shake off the shackles — if only for their sake.

But after just two weeks in hospital I foolishly opted to complete the course as an out-patient, and it was many more years before I came to fully realise that half measures are not nearly enough.

On my last day as an in-patient I had to present a reprise of my drinking history and the impact it was having on myself and those closest to me. It was a gruelling chore, writing and presenting that searching confession — titled 'Reality' — and I felt wiped out but strangely cleansed when I sat down after sharing my piece with the doctor, counsellor and fellow patients in group therapy.

But then, when the presentation was over, I bucked all professional advice — much rest having been the prescription — by bolting into town to attend a press conference for the Dublin City Marathon.

I managed to stay clean and sober for a few months and for a time was quite contented doing simple things like pushing a buggy or walking to the shops. But all too soon the old insecurities resurfaced and I was back reaching for the only things that would calm my restless spirit — the high stool and the well pulled pint.

I was into my 46th year and living in isolation in a little rented house near Lacken, in the Wicklow Hills, when I reached the rock bottom of despair. It was the night when my friend Ray McManus, of Sportsfile Photography fame, spotted me driving up Harold's Cross Road in the dark with no headlights or sidelights.

Ray is an award-winning photographer but could surely have been an ace detective or even a psychologist, because that night he brought the skills of both vocations to bear in a rapid-response operation I still marvel at.

I was heading back to Lacken that night with little or no hope left in my heart. I had let lapse the lease on the mountain cottage and was to vacate the place on the morrow by strict instruction of the landlord, and as I drove blindly into the dark I was in deep and dangerous confusion

Halfway up Harold's Cross Road the phone rang — pulling me from the pit of grim resolve. At first I ignored the irritation and drove on, but the ringing persisted and I pulled over to the kerb to zap the annoyance.

I always say it must have been the grace of God or my mother's prayers or both, because instead of hitting the OFF key I inadvertently hit ANSWER — and on the other end of the line heard Ray calling out in seeming desperation: 'Frank, Frank, I need you! I need you to help me, Frank! Something has happened and I'm in an awful state!'

'Jesus, what's the problem?' I enquired, my mind immediately switching from self-pity mode to concern for my great friend's distress.

'Where are you, Frank? Is there any way you could meet me at all?' he pleaded, the voice shaking with emotion.

'I'm not far from your house,' I replied, now totally focused on some kind of rescue mission.

'Pull in to your office up the road then and I'll call up and explain the problem,' he said.

Soon I was sitting upstairs in my office — the lease on which was also about to expire — and within minutes Ray rang the bell and entered. I was surprised and massively relieved to see that he looked okay — not nearly as distressed or dishevelled as I had been led to fear.

'What's the problem, Ray? What's happened at all?' I enquired — and was astonished as I watched his face break into a broad smile.

'I'm all right, Frank,' he said, standing close to me and looking me right in the eye. 'I'm all right, but I want to know what's the matter with you. Are you all right?'

That's when the dam broke in a torrent of tears as I poured my heart out to Ray, who just sat with me and listened.

'You're not alone,' he said, and those few words brought amazing comfort and relief.

'Let's go,' he said, after I told him I was about to become homeless in the hills. 'Let's go on out there now and get all your stuff sorted out.'

We drove to Lacken in Ray's car, and I was too exhausted to talk on the way. Inside the little house in the mountains Ray went into whirlwind mode and soon my worldly possessions were stacked in the boot and on the back seat of his car.

I still marvel at Ray's presence of mind that night on Harold's Cross Road, to work his brilliant brand of reverse psychology on me. He knew instinctively that if he tried in the obvious way to reel me in by asking straightaway what was wrong I might bolt, putting pedal to metal for fear of facing whatever demons I was running from.

Ray could always, and still can, read me like a book, and I believe he saved me from serious harm or worse on that crazy night.

There would be another chapter and another day of crisis further down the road in which Ray would again play a central role, a day when I finally saw the writing that had been so long on the wall in front of me.

But back to that night in Lacken. When we had pulled together my bits and pieces and were loaded and ready for the road back to Dublin, Ray had only a few words to say, words of deep kindness from a man who can often present a gruff exterior: 'There's a bed made up for you at the house and you'll be staying with us until you get back on your feet.'

He drove me to his home in Harold's Cross, where his wonderful wife, Anne, had tea and cake waiting. The tears I cried before going to sleep in a warm bed that night were tears of pure gratitude for a True Blue Dub with a heart as big as his native city and a unique understanding of the human condition.

49

Seeing The Light

And I ploughed on like the blind, regardless of a fall;
And I constantly ignored the writing on the wall.

IT was two years after I hit the half-century that I finally saw the writing on the wall that for years had been staring me in the face. Just as Mick Hanly put it in those powerful lyrics, I had ploughed on regardless.

I had made countless promises to myself to sober up entirely and return to regular running, and in the process I recalled numerous times certain lines from a ballad by Jim Dowling, a good friend and feature writer with *Irish Runner*.

Big Jim had penned those lines in the context of a cross-country race in the Phoenix Park on a day of wind, rain and mud. I wish I had kept the full narrative, describing as it did in colourful terms the trials of the long-distance runner negotiating switchbacks and pitfalls while 'doing the left-footed, two handed, side-sideways waltz.'

It felt a lot like that for me when I looked back at the decade preceding my 52nd birthday. I had made my life a big struggle. It was as if I were addicted to struggling rather than flowing and — to borrow from my mother — 'standing in my own light'. I was blocking the light that was there for me. I was fighting the flow.

One thing I knew for sure was that I had become addicted to alcohol — especially the comfort and escape it offered in times of stress and depression. I had tried on several occasions to quit and had received lots of help in Alcoholics Anonymous and from recovering alcoholics now leading lives of contented sobriety.

I'd make many efforts to stay off the drink, but it was always the old story of half measures achieving very little. Soon I was back on a barstool again, telling stories and singing songs while secretly dying inside.

Con Houlihan used to say we all have three dimensions — the public self, the private self and the secret self. That seemed to describe me perfectly.

And I would say even close friends hardly suspected the extent of my drinking or the violence of my mood swings. I tried in particular to hide matters from the kids when they were younger, but of course Marian was well aware of the impact on the family and on our relationship.

When I see my son Tomás now with his total hands-on approach to parenting, it makes me ashamed of how little I contributed when our own kids were small. It hits home especially hard when I call on the phone of an evening and his partner, Emer, tells me he's giving young Thomas and Luke their bath or putting them to bed. It reminds me how often I was marked absent when our children were little — always preoccupied elsewhere.

I continued to function and keep the magazine afloat but felt like a fraud when I wrote about the joy of running — a joy I had more or less abandoned. I would get back sporadically to running but could never sustain the effort.

Whenever I weaned myself briefly off alcohol, I would close up like a clam and be impossible to reach, wrestling with the darkness of depression and without the familiar crutch.

I was loath to discuss depression because I feared ending up emotionally crippled like my father. The fact that as I grew up we could never discuss his depression at home had left me with feelings of shame that would last for many years until I came to understand better what he had been going through.

I had found from an early age that alcohol could cover over fault lines I believed were part of my make-up. I was constantly on the run, but the things I ran away from were of my own making.

I listened to stories in AA rooms and marvelled at the apparent serenity of long-time AA members who had come to believe in a higher power and found the strength to change.

I could see at AA that there was no such thing as a hopeless case and that I was not alone in suffering from this soul-sickness. When I heard reformed alcoholics 'sharing' the reality of their loneliness, terror and pain, I identified and felt consoled. Even when I was at my lowest, there was always a sense of hope at those meetings. There was also great wisdom — though it took a long time for that wisdom to penetrate my cluttered mind.

I sat in an AA room on a September evening and thought how nice Christmas and the New Year would be and I sober for a change — never grasping that contented sobriety had to be earned one day at a time and that self-will was a lethal weapon you could turn on yourself.

In retrospect, I can see I was very much absorbed with self. I was also consumed by fear — a fear that I kept hidden but was always bubbling just below the surface.

I would run everything to the line — and am still very capable of doing that. I was big on procrastination and minuscule on planning, especially when it came to producing magazines. I'd always somehow pull rabbits out of hats with a last-gasp effort, and I expected others to tolerate my chaotic ways and keep faith with me. In essence, I was a troubled soul and had long been such.

There were rare times when I would open up to Marian — but always when I had alcohol on board. Then the shutters would come down and I'd be off again, in a welter of self-doubt and fear that the balls I was juggling would all come crashing to earth. And all the while the voice in my head kept replaying that old refrain of my mother's: 'Can you not do anything right?'

Despite all the inner turmoil, I had a good connect and a lot of fun with our kids — Tomás, Catherine, Conor, Laura and Claire — but I was mostly oblivious to Marian's heroic efforts to keep the family show on the road. To paraphrase a line from a great Mick

Hanly song — The Writing on the Wall — I listened to her dreams with one ear on the shelf.

I kept on selfishly plunging forward, in my more delusional moments even telling myself that alcohol was not only the best medication for depression but also a reasonable reward for long and unsocial working hours.

It had been the same drill back in Tennessee, especially in that last year when the dream had died and I was just scraping by. I would perch on the barstool in Sammy's Apex and join in the lively banter of 'good ol' boys' glorying in names like Jughead, Hotshot and Colonel, some of them cynical veterans of the Korean War.

Sammy Collins, the proprietor, would hand me a stack of quarters and say, 'Frank, it's your turn to play the jukebox.' I'd stack up then with a tear-jerking selection from Hank Williams, Willie Nelson, Kris Kristofferson, Waylon Jennings and Johnny Cash and wallow in self-pity and beer. Sammy and I were kindred spirits; we could have written songs on the subject of lonesome — and in fact we did.

Neil Cusack told me recently that I was into my second year at ETSU when it first occurred to him I was heading off on a tangent. He saw the change when I started hanging out with David McClellan and other questing spirits. By then I was replacing the disappointments and frustrations of a running career that had not lived up to expectations with immersion in a world of creative writing and music — a world in which alcohol was seen as an acceptable and even necessary creative tool.

And yet I somehow managed to bring each of our five children to America on different occasions and they got to visit our cousins in New York. And there were many great times we shared that I wouldn't trade, and numerous family photo albums bear testimony.

When my relationship with Marian foundered in the mid-1990s and my business partnership ended abruptly around the same time I found myself adrift in a sea of despair. I had tested

Marian's patience to the limit and so we became another fractured family statistic.

I felt lost, and the only thing I was able to salvage from the business split was *Irish Runner* magazine, which I steadfastly refused to let go of.

Separation from Marian and the kids was heartbreaking and I could only blame myself. Mick Hanly's song had further resonance for me, as I suspect it has had for many who have struggled with alcohol: *'We hurt the ones we love, to see how they will bend/ Push our luck so far, that we break them in the end/ And the day that we wake up, they have gone without recall/ Because we couldn't see the writing on the wall.'*

It was around that time that I headed for the Wicklow hills, foolishly believing I could somehow renew myself there in isolation and eventually find my way back home. I imagined that in a rented house in Lacken I might rediscover the peace and inspiration I had experienced at Wart Root Farm, a little oasis in the hills bordering Tennessee and Virginia.

In my last year in Tennessee Tanya Dennis — fiddle player and songwriter — brought me to Wart Root Farm, away off the beaten track and owned by Ken Marion, who would also become a lifelong friend.

That little house remains among my sweetest spots on earth and is always the place I head for when I get the chance to visit Tennessee. My sons, Tomás and Conor, have been to Wart Root Farm with me and witnessed the transformation that seems to occur when I bound down the hill and leap over the little stream there.

I found extraordinary peace there when on summer days I would sit for hours on the front porch, lulled by the hum of insects and feeling blissfully at one with myself and the world. By evening I would walk down to the big meadow, watch hawks floating on the thermals and return to the house to write poems and songs in a journal I kept for the purpose.

Wart Root Farm was a port of call for a range of colourful and engaging characters — mostly musicians, writers and artists who wandered in, assured of a welcome by Ken Marion. During winter I loved to sit in front of the pot-bellied stove as the wind howled in the trees outside.

I was into a seam of what I believed to be good writing at the farm and had a fair body of work building. Then I left the bag with all my precious scribblings on the seat of a pick-up truck that had given me a ride from the farm back to Johnson City. Distraught, I tried but failed to trace the driver. I often wonder what he made of all the pages he found in that battered shoulder bag — maybe he read and enjoyed at least some of them.

I laugh now when I recall how often I hitched in the dark of night from Johnson City to Wart Root Farm, usually starting out from Sammy's Apex. It was a fair journey but I always managed to get there — often thanks to a succession of short lifts. And of course I encountered plenty of offbeat characters among those kind enough to stop for me.

That year of 1976 I also hitched to Philadelphia after missing the bus taking the ETSU team to the NCAA Championships there. I might not have bothered but I had a newspaper assignment to cover the championships and so felt honour bound to get there.

After the first day of hitching I went under a bridge near the Pennsylvania Turnpike, put my duffel bag on the ground for a pillow and lay down. I was sleeping soundly when at around 4am I was rudely awoken by the beam of a great searchlight and a megaphoned command that brooked no argument: 'Come out with your hands up!'

I stumbled out into the light to be confronted by two well armed police officers — and was then astonished to observe another, and then another, vagrant emerge sheepishly from the shadows near where I had lain.

As my companions of the tunnel were being bundled into the

cop car it took all my powers of persuasion — and no little bit of Blarney — to stave off arrest. It always helped to be Irish in such situations, because someone or other was sure to have Irish roots, however far back.

When one of the cops asked me if I knew County Cork I told him it was virtually my back garden and furthermore I was probably on drinking terms with his distant cousins.

Soon I was allowed resume my slumbers: 'Go back in there and rest up,' said my newfound pals, 'but don't let us catch you hitching on the turnpike in the morning.'

Then they got in the car and with blue lights flashing took my erstwhile travelling companions away to an uncertain fate.

I have since wondered was I hopelessly naive or fearless or both back then, because I hardly thought of the dangers and just seemed to take experiences like that in my stride.

It was up at dawn and within minutes had secured a ride in a big truck that took me all the way to Philadelphia. For the return journey I enjoyed the luxury of a seat in the team bus.

When I moved out of the family home to the rented cottage in Lacken, I thought to recreate the idyll of Wart Root Farm. There was a big hill behind the house in Lacken and I vowed I would climb that hill every day. I would write and run and walk and renew my weary spirit until eventually Marian welcomed me home. I was only deluding myself.

There was one big problem — the pub was less than half a mile away. And so brokenhearted and still absorbed in my own woes, I lived in isolation for a while but never got to climb my promised hill of salvation.

I got on my feet again for a while after the night Ray McManus saw me driving without lights on Harold's Cross Road and pulled me back from the brink. But it was only a temporary reprieve, and I thrashed along for a few more years, barely keeping my head above water.

On a new year's day at that time, while lodging with a friend,

I was recovering from a night of heavy drinking and singing in the local pub.

My good friend by then well aware of my downward spiral, came in, handed me a white towel and said, 'Do you think you could take that towel, Frank, and throw it into the corner as a symbol of your willingness to turn over a new leaf in this new year?'

I took the towel, but could not bring myself to throw it. I had lost the will to make a fresh start.

Things came to a head again following my 51st birthday, when after several moves I was renting a house in Lucan and still keeping *Irish Runner* afloat but by the skin of my teeth and the help of good friends.

I would head back to the house — I never referred to it as home — of an evening and stop off at Courtney's thatched pub for 'two drinks at most'. But that two drinks stretched to many pints, especially on evenings when there was a good sing-song moving. I would have to leave the car at the pub overnight and this was happening four and five times a week.

Around this time I made a few trips back to St Patrick's Hospital, where Dr Matt Murphy, a man well versed in the human condition, listened to me with amazing patience and understanding. But every time he suggested I return to St Patrick's for a month as an in-patient I sidestepped — pleading work commitments and impending deadlines.

Then came a day when I could no longer sustain the charade. I looked Dr Murphy in the eye and told him I would submit to a treatment programme. The good doctor smiled and assured me I had finally made the right decision.

Making that decision brought massive relief. And so on a morning high on emotion, Ray McManus drove me to St Patrick's. Entering the hospital I suddenly felt overwhelmed and was on the verge of backing out, but my great friend and brilliant psychologist kept reins on me as I waited to sign in.

I intended keeping a firm grip on my laptop and phone so I could take the work into hospital with me, and was distraught to be told that those two extensions of my working self were barred during treatment. Ray had to almost physically wrest the phone from me and I felt naked and powerless without it.

Who would deal with the messages and the calls and the print deadlines? Would people think I had emigrated or that the magazine had folded? I could see that Ray was quietly amused by my panic, but the fact was that those two digital accessories had become crutches — part of my obsessive behaviour — and what body and mind really needed now was total rest.

As it transpired, Ray visited me every day in the hospital and did a firefighting job at *Irish Runner* in my absence. And what followed were four weeks when for once I did what was suggested to me by Dr Murphy and his staff.

That month began, however, with a weekend of the blackest depression I had ever suffered, something deep and primal, a massive sense of long-unresolved anguish that was choking me.

Somehow I survived, and when I went on the Monday to see Karen, my counsellor, it was as if some enormous dam had burst inside me once I had come off the treadmill of work and alcohol that had kept me propped up for so long.

All the sense of loss I had avoided facing for many years had hit home. I was grieving most for the great fighting spirit I had once had — a spirit that had been almost broken by the years of drinking and fleeing from reality.

I was grieving too for my parents in a deep and spiritual way as never before — remembering them with passionate love and understanding and grieving for their lives and their struggles.

I recalled with agonising clarity the last time I had spoken, on the phone from Dublin, to my father. He was in Swinford hospital and, with only hours to live, his voice was weak and plaintive.

'The last time.' Those are the cruellest three words in any language, and I remembered too the last time I drove my mother to Dublin on her final trip to St Luke's Hospital. It was a winter evening of relentless rain as we drove down the hill into Leixlip and the final miles to Rialto, both knowing, but unable to express it, that there would be no return journey to Mayo.

Dean Justice, a writer and friend back in the Tennessee hills, used to say I knew more about finality than anyone alive — and when I remembered my mother's final days in St Luke's I was inclined to agree.

I visited on a Christmas morning not long before her passing. I had been sober for a while and could see she was well pleased with my progress.

'Look after your children, Francis — that's my only request to you on this Christmas morning,' she said, smiling with wonderful serenity and amazing acceptance of her worsening condition. She was holding on for the return from Australia of my brother, Tom, and it was only when he arrived at the end of December that she was ready to let go and embrace death.

It was around midnight on January 4, and I had just arrived home from a hospital visit, when Tom called to say that our mother had died. He was with her at the end and she had passed peacefully.

Her body was brought back to Ballyhaunis on a treacherous day of snow and ice, and the undertaker suggested that for safety reasons he drive the hearse to Mayo without the usual convoy of mourners' cars.

And so we followed as far as Kilmainham and watched in a blinding flurry of falling snow as the hearse disappeared out of sight on the road westward. My mother was going home alone again — just as on the day all those years ago when, carrying her little bundle of new life, she boarded the train from Dublin back to Devlis.

Fr Tom — my brother was still an Augustinian priest — had presided over a lovely service at the hospital and we would later as a family follow my mother home for her funeral Mass and burial, with my father, in the graveyard near Drimbane, less than a mile from the village where they were born.

I had never fully grieved for my parents until that weekend of isolation in St Patrick's. I grieved too for lost friends and wasted years and for the running talent I had frittered away in Tennessee as I recklessly chased other dreams.

There was healing in the grieving, but it would take years for me to fully understand that in order to break through I had to first break down. In the desolation of the moment, the breaking down seemed more like coming apart, and the morning I visited Karen I felt the slender threads holding me together were unravelling all at once.

All my strength drained away, even my legs betraying me, and as Karen and a nurse accompanied me back to Laracor Ward they had to prop me up as I tottered and stumbled.

It was then a good friend, John Foley, appeared in a doorway.

'How are you Frank?' John asked, his face a picture of shock and puzzlement.

Unable to offer a coherent reply, I pointed to my counsellor and blurted, 'You'll have to ask her,' before staggering on toward the ward.

Many years on, John is CEO, and my boss, at Athletics Ireland, and we can laugh over a cup of tea in recalling that strange day when I seemed in a totally other world.

Later that morning it was decided I should move, for my own safety, to a locked ward. Laracor had an open regime reserved for patients who would soon be leaving the hospital, but there were other wards for those needing more careful oversight. You had to abandon your street clothes entering those lock-up wards and were likely to be on strong sedatives.

As I waited at the desk to be signed into Delaney Ward I looked inside and noticed people lying listless in their beds, some in the foetal position. I was gripped with a new terror. What if I ended up like them, drugged to the gills and without hope of recovery? I might be still there at Christmas, and way beyond.

And so I dug the heels in and fought a rearguard battle with staff, and it needed all that remained of my frazzled mental resources, and over two hours of pleading, to persuade them to bring me back to Laracor. I believe the winning of that battle was an important step on my road to recovery.

I have always believed too that it was my mother's spirit that enabled me at that time to hand over my life and my will to a higher power — a first step on the road to contented sobriety.

When four weeks later I signed out of St Patrick's I felt much stronger in mind and body but still a bit frayed and fragile. And despite everything, I reverted to type on my first weekend back on the street; I headed for London and a press reception for a running-shoe company that included a boat trip on the Thames with lavish food and drinks laid on. It was a crazy move and could have ended in disaster, but I made it and managed to avoid the eye of the wine waiter.

I arrived back at Dublin airport on a freezing night and on exiting the arrivals hall suddenly remembered I was actually homeless. I had once again let a lease expire, this time on the house in Lucan, and all my goods and chattels were stored temporarily in a house recently vacated by the McManuses in Kimmage.

It was then that the phone rang and up popped the name of Ray McManus. He and Anne were on the way back from Clare, the kettle would soon be bubbling, and a nice warm bed awaited me at their new home in Harold's Cross.

It was a lovely invitation but I turned it down, opting instead to head for the empty house in Kimmage. It was just something I needed to do, sleep there without heat or light. I was only a step away from being homeless, and this might give me some perspective on that condition and perhaps deepen my gratitude for what I still had.

I slept little that night, tossing and turning to keep warm, and was glad the following day to avail of Ray's offer of a bed and a short respite before I started to get back on my feet.

You might ask why I did not lift the phone to seek help from

Marian during those turbulent times. We were still in close touch and Marian and the children did visit me in hospital. But, just as during rough times in Tennessee, I wanted at all costs to hide the worst of my trauma from loved ones.

Today I am happy to say that Marian and myself are back on the one page. As I've worked on these chapters she has read many of them and liked what she read. We have even been able to laugh and cry a little at some of the memories. It's as if the writing of this memoir has somehow helped to bring us full circle as a family.

The past 12 years have in no way been easy, but they have, with the help of AA, family and friends, been years of total sobriety. And during that time I finally admitted to having struggled a lifetime with depression and sought help too in that area.

When I at last plucked up the courage to tell Dr Tony Crosbie of those struggles, he smiled and said, 'After nine years as your GP, I'm delighted to hear you admit that. We can start to do something about it now.'

It took several more years of prescribed medication to get me running in a straight line and today I am mostly free of the greyness that stalked me for so long.

'You fought a heroic battle with depression for many years,' my good friend Dr Murphy told me, and I suppose he had a point.

After I left hospital there was a nice twist — in every sense of the word — to my relationship with Dr Murphy. It happened on a wet Christmas morning at the GOAL Mile in Belfield.

That charity run proved my toughest physical effort in 21 years — my time of eight minutes and 20 seconds was over a minute slower than what I had done the previous year — but I was happy with an outing that had been necessarily tentative. And so it was in reflective mood that I jogged the perimeter of the track shouting occasional encouragement to friends making their own seasonal efforts for the Third World.

With thoughts of turkey and sprouts kicking in, I was about to call it a Christmas Day when to my surprise I noticed Dr Murphy on the track, giving the mile his best shot. 'Brilliant!' I thought. What more affirmative end to my year than to join him on the final lap of his odyssey?

And so on the top bend I gave a joyous bound onto the track and in my rush of enthusiasm forget the kerb was wet and slippy. At first I thought the stabbing pain in my right ankle was just a sprain, but the instant swelling and mounting agony confirmed I had done serious damage.

Lisa O'Shea swooped like an angel of mercy and soon we were heading for nearby St Vincent's Hospital accompanied by Brian Price and Greg Allen, long-time friends and supporters.

The diagnosis confirmed a fracture that required a cast for six weeks. A planned trip to see Tom in Australia three days later was suddenly on ice and for just a few moments I felt I had been hit by a train.

But there was a brighter side to that story. I soon discovered to my astonishment a calm acceptance of the misfortune, something I believe greatly accelerated the healing process and helped me measure my time in more precious units.

Virtually immobilised, I came to appreciate simple things like making a cup of tea while manoeuvring on crutches, negotiating the stairs, or simply asking help from strangers and being grateful to receive the same.

Being laid up at that time I was reminded of something another friend from Tennessee, Elizabeth Hunter, wrote in a beautifully reflective essay titled Gift of Days: 'My biggest lack, it seemed to me, was time to enjoy the life I had designed. I was squandering my gift of days and that gift is really our only one. We hope for other things — abiding love, children who turn out well, financial security, respect of our peers, and a home we love. But we cannot count on those. We can count only on our gift of days.'

There was another lovely sequel to the story of my fractured ankle when a few months later my son Tomás enquired if I still intended visiting Australia.

'I've shelved the idea for now,' I told him.

'No you haven't, Dad,' he replied. 'You're going there in a couple of months' time and I'm going with you.'

And so Tomás and I got to spend three rare and unforgettable weeks in Sydney with Tom and his wife, Cathy — Tom having by then left the priesthood.

A few months later I met Dr Murphy and recounted my GOAL mile misadventure. He had continued on his way that Christmas morning and finished his charity run blissfully oblivious. We laughed when we talked of the accident and its aftermath — further evidence of how things can come full circle in the most surprising ways.

50

The Power Of Three

THERE are three wonderfully endearing companions with whom I have had the privilege to travel to athletics events at home and abroad: the Three Amigos — Sean Callan, Harry Gorman and Matt Rudden.

In 2016, God willing, Harry will embark on his 15th straight Olympic voyage in a series that began with a trip to Rome in 1960.

A former national champion over a range of distances from two miles to marathon, Harry, the eldest of the three, has had a lifelong passion for running. At age 85, he continues to train four times a week in the Phoenix Park.

It was the Moscow Olympics that brought the Three Amigos together as a travelling party, and the bond has remained unbroken.

They knew each other well before that; they had been clubmates at St Augustine's in Dublin. But Moscow kicked off a series of global adventures that have taken them to all five continents supporting Irish athletes at Olympics, World Championships, European Championships on track and country, and big city marathons — the whole calendar of international competition.

Sean Callan is the acknowledged team leader and unofficial travel agent. A native son of Ardee, Sean was a raw and exciting young talent back in the 1950s. Old stagers in County Louth still speak in awe of his early cross-country exploits. In 1957 he won the National Youths title. In 1958 he added the National Junior title to his growing list of victories and, at just 19, finished third to the legendary Willie Morris in the National Senior Cross Country in Athenry.

Sean was, like myself, a disciple of the great Emil Zatopek and, when with Ferdia AC in Ardee, was often observed running alone, wearing heavy army boots, along the railway line and for miles out into the Louth countryside.

Sean was more than a fine runner; he was blessed with the gift of conviviality. And he has made good use of it, winning friends wherever he goes. Travel with him to a major event abroad, be it Olympics or World Championships, and you are constantly being introduced to acquaintances he has made in every far-flung athletics outpost of the planet.

Matt Rudden, like Sean, also once claimed bronze — behind Sean O'Sullivan and Johnny Downes — in the National Senior Cross Country. He competed for Laragh AC in Cavan before emigrating to Dublin and is the man whose Rudden Brothers construction company built the magnificent Donore Harriers Sports Centre in Chapelizod.

Matt is the quiet man of the trio. But he too is steeped in athletics. For good measure, he is also an easy mixer and a perfect, gentle foil for his two more ebullient companions.

Harry Gorman is the flag bearer, figurative and literal, of the Three Amigos and has appeared in full Irish regalia on TV screens and in national newspapers during several Olympiads. He seldom fails to get into the picture when Irish athletes are celebrating international success.

A man of endless good cheer, he revels in meeting people — and in tales of the unexpected. He recalls, for instance, how the Three Amigos landed on their feet at the 1980 Olympics, when they ended up staying in a hotel that had been booked for the US track and field team, which had been prevented by the boycott from travelling.

Harry loves his food almost as much as his athletics, and he fondly recalls the cuisine laid on for the Irish during that Moscow experience, when himself, Sean and Matt 'lived like kings' and were chauffeured daily to and from the stadium.

Not surprisingly, there have been hiccups along the way, but the Amigos have always emerged intact — no doubt their own irrepressible good nature has been a factor.

Matt, for instance, had a potential nightmare at the 1988 Seoul Olympics when Sean hurried off to attend the track events, forgetting to give Matt his stadium tickets. To compound the problem, Matt found himself alone in the teeming city, unsure which hotel they had booked into and without ready cash.

But for the kindly intervention of a lady at the Olympic help desk, who called dozens of hotels on his behalf, the Cavanman might well have found himself temporarily living rough in Seoul.

That Korean woman who befriended Matt would later visit Ireland and meet the lads on their home patch.

The Three Amigos are recognised at home and abroad. They have long been on first-name terms with most of Ireland's elite athletes, spanning several generations, as well as a host of international stars. They have supported Irish athletes through good times and difficult. They have celebrated in Los Angeles, Gothenburg, Sydney, Paris, Beijing and London, but have also kept faith in fields and stadia where our athletes were eclipsed. They have also, over many years, been the most reliable and willing of volunteers at road, track and cross-country events throughout the land.

They will probably sit together on the plane to the Rio Olympics in 1916, and when they get there they will bring palpably more colour and camaraderie to what should be another great feast of athletics.

51

Priest On The Run

KNOWN affectionately to his friends as 'Galloping Jesus', he's a man of boundless energy and enthusiasm — as well as a lifelong passion for athletics. I have been fortunate over the years to have travelled with Fr Liam Kelleher to numerous events, including a couple of Olympiads, and the experience has never been less than memorable.

To say that the Cork curate — who these days ministers in Cobh, the hometown of Sonia O'Sullivan — is larger than life would be a lame understatement.

For as long as I have known him, Fr Liam has seemed in perpetual motion. When he was attached to the parish of Tullylease, in East Cork, the question would often be asked in affectionate jest: What is the difference between God and Fr Liam? The answer: God is everywhere but Fr Liam can be found everywhere except the parish of Tullylease.

Another popular saying back then was that if you parked for an hour at any crossroads in East Cork, Liam Kelleher was sure to drive past.

Fr Liam has coached countless champions and continues to worker tirelessly, coaching and encouraging youngsters.

I have great memories of the Dromina 10 that he organised back in the early 1980s, a road race that attracted the cream of distance talent. Any project involving Fr Liam gets his total focus and massive energy, and so it was with the Dromina classic, where Jerry Kiernan's 46:30 was, and remains, one of the great all-time road runs.

Another Fr Kelleher brainchild — the track in Tullylease — earned him international note when on one occasion that entered athletics folklore he used his truly unique communication and persuasion skills to bring mile legends such as Eamonn Coghlan, Steve Ovett, John Walker, Frank O'Mara and Ray Flynn all together to race there.

Two years before that historic track meeting, he had cajoled Steve Ovett to cut the ribbon and officially open the track carved from the side of a hill.

In one of Fr Liam's more novel fundraising ideas to bring the dream to fruition, he ran 150 laps (37 miles) around the track, then nearing completion, on St Patrick's Day 1979. Every child who raised a fiver in sponsorship for that run received a free pass to the World Cross Country in Limerick later that month, and anyone who raised a tenner got a free bus-ride, as well as a ticket, to the event.

The construction of the track in Tullylease cost around £20,000 in old money and Fr Kelleher's 150-lap solo odyssey raised a quarter of that amount.

Travelling in the company of Fr Liam Kelleher has always been massively enjoyable and never boring. Several incidents still make me smile. One such was at the Atlanta Olympics in 1996.

I was sitting in the press stand a couple of days into those Olympics when the good priest instructed me to follow him to another part of the stadium, insisting, 'I have a much better seat for you,' and making a beeline down to trackside, right by the finish line.

'There are two seats in there that nobody has been using and I hate to see them going to waste,' Liam said.

The vacant seats were in the corporate area and it transpired that Fr Liam himself had been occupying one of them for the past two days.

'Sit down there, enjoy the view and don't attract any attention to yourself,' he said.

For the rest of the week I had a close-up view of all the track action, and Liam and myself were within touching distance of the athletes as they were interviewed by TV crews immediately after their events.

A couple of seats away, a huge American wielding a large camcorder got tremendously excited every time Michael Johnson was in action. As soon as the sprint superstar crossed the finish line in a qualifying round, the fan would be on his feet, waving and roaring: 'Michael, Michael! Over here, Michael! Look over here!'

Of course the loud American was drawing a lot of attention to himself, and one day during a lull in the track action a security man singled him out for questioning.

'Excuse me, Sir,' the security man said, looking directly at our noisy neighbour. 'Would you mind if I enquired how much this corporate seat cost you?'

'Hell, the seat I'm sitting in didn't cost me a dime,' answered the big man. 'It was a corporate gift to my company from Bausch and Lomb.'

The security man then turned his focus on Fr Liam: 'Sir, can you tell me how much your seat cost?'

Quick as a flash, Fr Liam replied, 'It's the same as our friend beside me here. My seat is also a gift from Bausch and Lomb to my company back in Ireland.'

To my considerable relief, the security man gave up his quest for information and moved on.

It was at the Sydney Olympics that Fr Liam best demonstrated his powers of persuasion when against all the odds he managed to winkle out press accreditation on the day of the women's 5,000m final.

For a good few years while he was publisher and editor of *Marathon* magazine, Fr Liam had enjoyed official accreditation for a number of Olympiads, but he had failed to secure a press pass for Sydney. For several days he had tried from every angle to get his hands on the priceless piece of plastic that would give access to the press stand and mixed zone. Then, on the day of the 5,000m final, he asked me to accompany him to the press office, where he would give it one last throw of the dice.

I held little hope of success but I agreed to go with him as moral support, and soon we were seated together in the media accreditation office before a young lady with a shamrock tattooed on an ankle, something I knew Fr Liam had been quick to take in.

My friend skipped the formalities and got straight to the point.

'I just have to get into the stadium to see Sonia O'Sullivan in the 5,000-metre final,' he told the young woman.

'I'm a great friend of Sonia's and have followed her career since she was a youngster back in Ireland. I'm a good friend of Cathy Freeman's too, and she's running in the 400-metre final tonight.' Name-checking the great Australian could do no harm.

With that, Fr Liam tipped the contents of a shopping bag onto the desk and began leafing through back issues of *Marathon* magazine — much to the bewilderment of the young lady holding all the aces in terms of press accreditation.

'Look here, look here!' Liam told her. 'See Cathy Freeman here in *Marathon* magazine! She calls me Father.'

'You're joking of course,' the young woman smiled.

'No I'm not joking at all — Cathy calls me Father because I'm a Catholic priest and she gave me an interview for this magazine that I publish back in Ireland.

'You must know about Ireland too because I see you have a tattoo with the shamrock on your ankle. You'll have to help me because I just need to be in that stadium tonight.'

'Give me a few minutes to check with my boss,' the young lady said as she left us alone in her office. A few minutes later we watched her return up the hall, holding some papers in her hand.

'It's looking good — she has a form at least,' said my companion gleefully.

'I'm breaking all the rules here, but if you fill out this form quickly I'll get you organised,' the be-shamrocked lady said.

Soon Fr Liam had his ID photo taken and his official press pass dangling from his neck. It was then that I remembered that on this particular night, with three massive finals on the track — the women's 400m and 5,000m and the men's 10,000m — even accredited journalists would need a special admission ticket as well as the press pass.

'Ask her for the special ticket for tonight,' I urged Fr Liam.

'No, I've stretched my luck enough,' he said. 'Don't worry, Frank. Once I have the press pass I'll get into the stadium — that I can assure you.'

Security was especially tight as we approached the entrance to the stadium and I went up just ahead of Fr Liam to present my pass and special ticket for inspection.

Once admitted, I looked around to see if he had followed, but there was no sign of him. Then, as I made my way deeper into the stadium, he appeared out of the shadows and enquired with a cheeky grin, 'Which way is the press tribune, Frank?'

I have yet to figure out — I really must ask him — how the good and holy man beat the security system that night, but it was certainly not the first time, or the last, that he performed what many would have deemed a miracle.

It was after midnight in Sydney when Fr Liam and I met Sonia O'Sullivan under a street light at the far end of the Olympic Stadium and with cans of coke toasted her 5,000m silver medal.

It was a rich and rare moment for me, on that very special night, to be in the company of the Cobh Express and 'Galloping Jesus' himself.

52

Safety In Numbers

I MADE another return to running in 1988 when, having been roped by Frank Slevin into a fundraising crusade for Cerebral Palsy Ireland, I trained for about four months with the New York City Marathon in mind.

And it's still hard to believe that there we were on race morning in Lower Manhattan — five of us: Frank, Bertie Messitt, Frank Broughal, Niall Mathews and myself — and not a race number between us.

We were all reasonably fit and raring to run. We had logged serious training miles in the build-up, what was termed a 'major fundraiser' for the charity. But our leader, Frank Slevin of BHAA and Dublin Marathon fame, was not enjoying his first day in the Big Apple.

Frank had shepherded us to Race HQ in Manhattan confident we would be received as VIPs. After all, didn't we have an Irish Olympian and distance legend, Bertie Messitt, on our little team that had already raised £10,000 for Cerebral Palsy Ireland (provided we finished the race).

Frank had met Fred Lebow, New York Race Director, months earlier in Dublin and had secured a letter of invitation for our team to run in the great event. The letter, on official New York Marathon stationery, was effusive and, as intended, did wonders for our fundraising efforts.

Unfortunately for Frank and the rest of us, the letter cut no ice when it came to looking for our official race numbers. I can still see the flame-haired lady at the check-in desk — glorying in the lovely name of Terpsie Toon I seem to recall — look us up and down as we arrived to claim the numbers we assumed awaited us.

'When did you enter the race?' she demanded by way of introduction.

'We didn't have to enter at all,' Frank told her as he confidently slipped the 'Official Invitation' from Fred across the desk. Terpsie studied the letter and passed it back with a calm but firm reply.

'I'm sorry, Sir, but this just states that Mr Lebow would be happy to welcome you to the New York City Marathon. It says nothing about race entries, which are your own responsibility. Entries for this year's race closed months ago.

'Fred is not here right now and he hasn't issued any complimentary numbers for you, so you will not be able to run in the race this year.'

It was clear that Terpsie was not for turning, and panic set in. Bewildered, we scoured the huge Running Expo in search of Fred Lebow, who — Frank Slevin assured us — would cut through all the red tape.

'I'd do the same for him in Dublin,' said Frank.

We finally caught up with the elusive Fred striding down one of the aisles and our leader walked briskly alongside him explaining our dilemma.

'I was sure you had us entered,' Frank told the New York Marathon supremo, who was vigorously shaking his head.

'What are we going to do now?' asked Frank. 'We've raised 10,000 pounds for a charity back in Ireland and we all have to finish the New York Marathon.'

'Well I guess you'll have to give the money back,' suggested Fred without breaking stride. That's when the real panic set in.

The following morning we were back, present and correct, at Race HQ, again pleading our case but again to no avail. Crestfallen, we retired to our hotel, all the while trying to figure out how we could break the bad news to Dermot Ward, CEO of Cerebral Palsy Ireland, who had come to New York to support us.

We were not long back in our hotel when we received a phone call from a *New York Daily News* reporter who had learned of our plight. Later in the afternoon we received another call requesting us to return to Race HQ. A limousine, we were told, was on its way to take us there.

It transpired that the previous day Niall Mathews, producer of RTÉ's *Fair City*, had a meeting with Adrian Flannelly, whose radio show had a huge Irish audience. Over a drink, Niall poured out his and our problem, and Flannelly in turn aired the story on his show. The news was picked up by a PR executive and advisor to New York Mayor Ed Koch, soon to be running for re-election.

The Mayor valued the New York Irish vote and wanted no negative publicity. A request went to Fred Lebow to get the problem sorted out before it gained legs, in a manner of speaking.

And so, courtesy of a police escort, we made it to the start and we all completed the New York City Marathon.

I will never forget my run through Central Park. I had hit the wall at 22 miles and my last four miles were a mixture of jogging and walking. I was wearing a colourful *Irish Runner* tee-shirt and every time I slowed to a walk I heard roars from the throngs lining the sidewalks: 'Come on, Irish, you can't stop now!'

I made my slow and painful progress to the finish and was rewarded with a time of 3 hours and 29 minutes, one of the most satisfying experiences of my life.

It's a few years since we bade our last farewell to the running legend that was Bertie Messitt, and when I think of him, as I often do, I always remember with great fondness that magical weekend in New York and recall the valuable lessons for life — and the marathon — I learned there.

Good preparation is vital, but more vital still is refusing to give up. It was a lesson that defined Bertie's life and his illustrious running career.

53

The Thrill Of Speed

THE 1988 New York Marathon story had a nice, if heart-stopping, sequel that involved Dermot Ward, CEO of Cerebral Palsy Ireland, and myself.

Dermot and I needed to return home the day after the race, while the rest of our group opted to stay on for a few days of sightseeing in the Big Apple. We were due to fly out of Kennedy Airport on the Monday evening but first had an important function to attend.

The year 1988 was Millennium time in Dublin and an arrangement had been made for Dermot and our group to present a special Dublin Millennium Candle to Mayor Ed Koch at City Hall. It was going to be a tight schedule, because the time for the function was set uncomfortably close to when Dermot and I needed to be heading for Kennedy.

And so we arrived at City Hall with plenty of time to spare, hoping the mayor would also be running a little ahead of his own busy schedule. Dermot Ward was especially anxious to make it back to Dublin; he had an important meeting on Tuesday and was checking his watch repeatedly from the moment we reached City Hall.

We received a great welcome from Ed Koch's staff, but to our dismay a PR executive informed us that the mayor would be behind, rather than ahead of, schedule.

'That's not a problem,' Dermot assured the PR man. 'A pair of us have a plane to catch at Kennedy and the rest of the guys here can make the presentation when the mayor arrives. Frank and I will just head out and hail a cab for the airport.'

The PR executive smiled and replied calmly but firmly, 'I'm sorry, Sir, but I believe Mayor Koch would like to meet your full visiting party and has arranged to have a photo taken with the whole group. I think it best we do not disappoint him. I can assure you that you will still get to the airport on time.

'In the meantime, while we're waiting for the mayor to arrive, I have arranged for a guide to show you around City Hall. Don't worry, Mayor Koch will soon be along and once we have the photo taken you can leave for Kennedy.'

Keen to avoid a diplomatic incident, we nodded in general agreement, and soon we were being led around City Hall by a friendly and highly informative guide who gave us the lowdown on the history of the famous landmark.

As we followed our guide I could see Dermot nervously checking his watch, clearly getting more anxious by the minute. I figured that by now our chances of making our Aer Lingus flight were slim — especially with the evening rush-hour traffic — and so I resigned myself to staying an extra night and booking a flight for Tuesday.

Dermot, however, had different ideas. A high-ranking Guinness executive before his retirement, he was totally committed to honouring business arrangements, and the thought of missing the important Tuesday meeting he had scheduled in Dublin was not to be entertained.

'I'm very sorry,' Dermot told the PR man when we completed our grand tour. 'We really have to go right now to have any chance at all of catching our plane.'

'The mayor will be here within minutes,' the PR man insisted. 'We must get the group photo taken, and don't worry, you'll get to Kennedy in good time.'

Beads of sweat forming on his forehead, Dermot paced up and down, still checking his watch. I could not fathom the repeated assurances of the PR man, because by now it seemed logistically impossible to reach the airport in time, even in the unlikely event we found a cab in the thick of evening rush hour. Having decided we would have to say overnight, I was relaxed about the situation, but Dermot was extremely unhappy and seemed on the verge of blowing a gasket.

The tension eased somewhat when Mayor Koch and his entourage swept into the building, greeted us like long-lost friends and offered apologies for the late arrival. Soon we were assembled for the group photo with the mayor and the Dublin Millennium Candle, though I'm not sure Dermot managed to crack a smile for the camera.

'I'm afraid a few of us have to leave now in a big hurry,' Dermot said as he shook Mayor Koch's hand. 'We have to get a cab to the airport.'

Koch smiled and, indicating his PR executive, said, 'I think that's all arranged, Dermot. I believe you have a car waiting out back.'

With that, the PR man and his staff grabbed our bags and rushed us to the back exit, where an NYPD Cruiser awaited with lights flashing.

'These boys will get you to Kennedy on time and the airline has been informed that you're on the way,' said the PR man, to Dermot's immense relief.

Dermot and I were quickly installed in the back seat and with sirens wailing we took off an a hair-raising and knuckle-whitening trip to Kennedy. Pinned by G-forces to the back of our seats, we hurtled through the tunnel that led toward the airport, while the cop in the passenger seat on his loudhailer warned traffic to make way for the Cruiser with the two Irishmen on board.

'Move over! Move over now!' was the message that cleared our path as if by magic.

Soon we screeched to a halt outside the building with the familiar Aer Lingus sign and with the help of our new NYPD buddies were fast-tracked to the Aer Lingus desk and the friendly assurance that we had just beaten the deadline.

Soon we were cruising at 39,000 feet — both still grinning ear to ear about our exhilarating experience.

A few days later back in Dublin I called Dermot to enquire how his meeting had gone on the Tuesday.

'It went like a dream,' he said. 'A great outcome entirely!'

'Have you thought any more about our trip to Kennedy?' I asked.

'I have indeed, Frank, and I have only one regret.'

'What's that?' I enquired.

'The only regret is that I did not have that experience when I was nine years old — because it was an experience to last a lifetime.'

54

Her Finest Hour

I HAVE been fortunate to have covered every summer Olympics since 1992, and *Irish Runner* has, courtesy of Pat Hickey, President of the OCI, been afforded official media accreditation since the 1984 Games in Los Angeles.

It has been wonderful covering these Olympiads, and the sweetest of all my Olympic experiences has to be Sydney 2000, when I also worked for the INN organisation that linked news and sports reports to most of Ireland's regional radio stations.

I worked a punishing schedule in Sydney, filing live reports from the mixed zone as Irish athletes emerged from competing in the stadium and doing follow-up stories on some of the many highlights each day. I found the whole thing hugely satisfying and marvelled at how easily I adapted to conducting live interviews on a Nokia mobile phone that had a microphone built into a little cover flap.

I pulled off a minor coup on the final day of those Games by securing a live interview with the great Ethiopian Haile Gebrselassie. But it is Tuesday night September 25 that remains most graphically etched in the memory — a night of extraordinary performances before a world-record crowd of 112,574.

It was of course the night that Sonia O'Sullivan showed all her resilience, raw courage and fighting spirit to secure the Olympic medal that had eluded her in Barcelona and Atlanta.

It was also the night Cathy Freeman struck 400m gold in front of her adoring home support and thereby somewhat eclipsed in euphoria much of the other drama on what was arguably the best night of athletics ever. Even the great Michael Johnson of the USA was reduced to a supporting role on this evening of heroics.

The three-hour pole-vault duel between Stacy Dragila of the US and Australia's Tatiana Grigorieva was absorbing enough to temporarily distract spectators and calm nerves in the build-up to Freeman's final — the former Russian repaying Australian investment by taking silver behind Dragila's gold.

There was still more drama in the 10,000m final, an epic replay of Atlanta 96 in which Haile Gebrselassie again showed perfect judgement to snatch gold from Paul Tergat of Kenya.

Naoko Takahashi's marathon win was declared one of the greatest runs ever over the classic distance; she broke the Olympic record by over 90 seconds on a course recognised as seriously tough.

But there was nothing to match the atmosphere generated by Freeman. And there was nothing to quite match her post-race comments: 'I could feel the crowd just totally around me, all over me. I could feel everyone's emotions, the happiness and joy absorbing into every pore of my body. I just had to sit down and make myself feel normal and get comfortable. It was beyond words.'

All the emotion was mutual. Even hardened newspaper hacks waxed poetic. 'Heroism And Grace Wrapped In A Precious Package,' screamed a headline in the *Sydney Morning Herald* the following day.

There was surely never before a single occasion when an Australian athlete carried so much national expectation.

Likewise, there was a huge burden of Irish expectation on Sonia O'Sullivan's slender shoulders. And this time, as many a time before, she responded, claiming precious silver and missing gold by half a stride while putting supporters, as many a time before, through a wringer of emotions.

Sonia suffered a crisis of confidence after Gabriela Szabo took the field through the first kilometre in 3:03.84. The Cobh

Express appeared to waver and drifted back to 11th place, conjuring for those of us in the press box nightmares of Atlanta 96 and other past disasters.

But Sonia loves nothing better than to surprise us, and that night in Sydney she clawed her way back into contention. Afterwards, she was at a loss to explain exactly what had happened.

'You know there was a point in the race when I was nearly gone,' she reminded us, as if we hadn't noticed, in the mixed zone under the stands. 'And then somehow I got myself back into it again — really into the race.'

Sonia's finish that night was as noble as she had ever delivered, and yet when 15 years later I reread her further comments, they revealed her vulnerability: 'There were points coming down the straight when I was really, really trying and there was nothing else I could do. It could have ended up similar to Barcelona because of the way things worked out, and people were so close at the end.'

The media area was a scene of unbridled joy. An army of Irish wellwishers had breached security to await Sonia's arrival. Pat Hickey was holding court, proudly sharing the news that he'd been invited to present the race medals, and I could not help thinking how sharp the contrast between here and Atlanta four years earlier when Sonia was on the floor.

Out in the stadium Sonia was still coming to terms with her achievement, circling the track, waving to a delirious Irish fan club that included, of course, the three ever-presents: Sean Callan, Harry Gorman and Matt Rudden.

She had to share her finest moment with Cathy Freeman as to thunderous applause the Australian icon was summoned to the rostrum for the 400m medal ceremony. It was certainly a night for goose pimples, a night to savour and give thanks and pinch oneself to make sure all that was happening was not a dream.

Sonia took forever to exit doping control and had to abandon a scheduled press conference. Her mother, Mary, and sister,

Gillian, waited patiently in the press room only to learn she had left the stadium and was on her way home.

Fr Liam Kelleher and myself joined the O'Sullivans searching for the woman of the moment. It was surreal, standing in the Olympic Stadium near midnight as one by one the lights were doused where a few hours earlier glorious pandemonium had reigned.

We went out into the night and walked with the O'Sullivans across the dark and almost deserted Olympic Park. Then a mobile phone sounded — Sonia was at large and looking for her family.

We met them a little after midnight — herself, Nick Bideau and Alan Storey — under a street light in the far corner of the park.

It was a simple and memorable meeting for everyone, but a brief one — Mary and Gillian were booked on a 5am flight to Brisbane. We got to see and touch the medal. Then Fr Liam commandeered a passing bus to take himself and myself to the train station en route back to our lodgings.

I celebrated with a Mars bar and a coke on the train and thought of a cross-country day many years before in Killenaule when the teenage Sonia first showed to a wide public the fabulous promise that had now been truly fulfilled. I thought too of the great resilience she had shown after her Atlanta nightmare, bouncing back with the determination and inner steel of a true champion.

It was a lovely ending to an extraordinary day and I felt blessed to have been part of it.

55

The Pure Drop

MY love of music and singing goes all the way back to childhood and the house dances and weddings I attended with my parents. I would sit enthralled watching the fiddler Joe Mannion playing at those intimate house gatherings.

I had heard it said that this great musician had courted my Aunt Dell before she left for America, and when she was leaving he gave her a gold medal he had won at the All-Ireland Feis. I heard my parents recall how broken-hearted Joe had been when my father's sister emigrated all those years ago. Little did I think that years later I would visit Aunt Dell in the Bronx or that I would finish writing a song celebrating her long life on the very day she died in New York at age 93.

I loved the music played on fiddle, concertina and accordion at those parties, and I especially loved watching the couples waltzing around the kitchen in sweet unison. Those were the times I felt particularly close to my parents, and I felt that closeness even more as we walked home together from such gatherings, my father in full flow of talk after several bottles of stout and my mother, a non-drinker, also in high spirits.

My father would not go to the pub on Saturday nights until his favourite radio programme, *The Ballad Makers*, had aired. It was a programme I too came to love, and soon my father's favourite songs — *Patrick Sheehan (The Glen of Aherlow)*, *Skibbereen*, *My Poor Dog Tray*, *The Moon Behind the Hill*, *Moonlight in Mayo* and suchlike — were part my own repertoire. I would learn the words by heart and sing them when nobody could hear.

Then, when Aunt Dell finally came back to visit her home place, I plucked up enough courage to sing her a few of those classics — a step on the road of a lifelong passion.

Music was very much part of my school and teenage years, and I would often on Saturday nights sneak into a bar in Ballyhaunis to hear Tony Rattigan — aka The Singing Cowboy — perform on a small stage to an appreciative audience.

During my early years in St Patrick's College, I longed to join up with music groups formed from time to time by friends, but anxiety and shyness always held me back.

My only venture into show business was when I was cast as Aunt Abby in a St Patrick's College performance of *Arsenic and Old Lace* produced by Fr Kiernan Waldron.

The show was warmly and widely acclaimed, and I suspect that first venture into acting was what eventually prompted me to consider majoring in Theatre at East Tennessee State — before I introduced Ray McBride to the discipline.

My passion for music was very much alive when I first moved to Dublin, and I was a regular at Sunday-morning traditional sessions in Slattery's of Capel Street and later in Meagher's Log Cabin in Fairview. I also frequented the dance halls — The Irish Club, The Ierne, The Olympic Ballroom — fortified usually with several pints of Guinness the better to overcome chronic shyness when it came to asking ladies onto the floor.

Meanwhile, out on the postal beat, I was like a moving jukebox, transistor blaring out the hits of the day from Radio Luxembourg or 'the songs our fathers loved' from the Waltons programme on Radio Eireann — 'If you feel like singing, do sing an Irish song,' was the programme catchline.

The ballad and folk scenes were in full flow, and I loved such popular venues as The Meeting Place, the Embankment and O'Donoghue's on Merrion Row.

When I moved to Dublin for the second time, in the late 1970s, I would often see one of my especial heroes, Luke Kelly, drinking in McDaid's of Harry Street. I never plucked up the courage to talk to Luke, but I revered the legendary balladeer.

One morning over drinks in McDaid's, Ray McBride and myself realised we were fast running out of funds sufficient to carry the session into the afternoon.

'We'll have to take drastic action or we'll have a very dry afternoon,' McBride said.

At that time, the 'holy hour' was still being observed, pubs being required by law to close doors between 2pm and 3pm. And so at two o'clock we ventured down Grafton Street and chose our pitch outside Bewley's 'legendary, lofty, clattery café', where McBride divested himself of his jacket and placed it at his feet.

'Let's give them a few ballads and hillbilly songs like we did back in Tennessee,' he said, and soon we were in full voice, McBride punctuating the show by breaking now and then into a lilting and electrifying burst of Irish dancing. An audience gathered and to our great delight coins started to land into the collection jacket.

We spent an enjoyable 'holy hour' busking on Grafton Street and our impromptu session yielded enough for us to provide McDaid's with our valued custom well into the night.

Back in Tennessee, McBride and I had formed a ballad group we called The Irish Rebels, and for lead musician, on guitar and squeezebox, we had the fastest Irish miler of all time, Ray Flynn from Longford.

McBride was Mr Versatility in the group — he could sing, play tin whistle and bodhrán, and for good measure dance like the Irish and World champion he was.

We had a dulcimer player too — a lovely American lass called Linda Sparks — and we were occasionally joined on stage by the young and brilliant Tanya Dennis from Johnson City on fiddle, a woman who would become a lifelong friend of mine.

Neil Cusack was noted for his lively rendering of *An Poc Ar Buile*, while I concentrated on more serious or soulful numbers such as *The Men Behind the Wire*, *Raglan Road*, and *Will You Go Lassie Go*.

We played plenty of small gigs on campus and around Johnson City, and our biggest claim to fame was probably the night we performed on stage in the famous Carter Family Store — now the Carter Family Fold — in Hiltons, Virginia, just across the border from Tennessee.

I had become good friends with Janette Carter and often visited the home of the legendary Carter Family on Saturday nights in the company of my great Texas friend Benny Patrick. Janette was the daughter of the famous AP Carter, and she and her brother Joe loved Irish music and song.

As for that night long ago, we played and sang our hearts out to a spellbound audience before McBride stole the show with an incredible display of both Irish dancing and Tennessee clogging.

On my final year in Tennessee, I would follow my musical passion through the mountains, meeting legends like the late and great singer Jean Richie and that wonderful brace of fiddlers JP Frawley and Tommy Jarrell.

It was Tanya Dennis who really fuelled my fascination with 'old time mountain music' during that final year. She took me one weekend to the Old Time Mountain Music Festival in Berea, Kentucky, and there I met another genius, the hammer dulcimer virtuoso and noted songwriter John McCutcheon.

Benny Patrick was also a big influence on my musical education in Tennessee. We were both huge fans of Willie Nelson, Waylon Jennings, Johnny Cash, Kris Kristofferson and John Prine.

Years later I met one of those musical heroes when I got to sit and chat for half an hour with Kristofferson in Dublin and had to keep pinching myself to be sure I wasn't dreaming.

I was fortunate to meet my favourite songwriter on two more occasions. And then to cap a lifetime of musical passion, I hit it lucky when the highly regarded folk singer Sean Tyrrell called me one day to say he would like to put music to lyrics I had written for him on a napkin in a pub two years previously.

Those few verses I titled Marian's Song, dedicated to my

beautiful wife, who, to paraphrase a Kristofferson song, 'saved me from the things I might have been'.

Marian's Song

You're feeling as bleak as the first days of winter,
And thinking that no one loves you at all;
An angel of lonesome is perched on your shoulder,
And your fragile emotions are now in freefall.

(Refrain)
Sit with me, talk with me, come then and walk with me,
Down by the ocean when it's high tide;
Let me help you unburden this feeling of lonesome;
I've been where you're anchored, let me be by your side.

These grey days of winter won't last forever,
And sunshine again will feel warm on your face;
You're brittle, not broken, just feeling neglected;
I've been where you're anchored, I've moored in that place;
I've been where you're anchored, I've moored in that place.

(Refrain)
Sit with me, talk with me, come then and walk with me,
Down by the ocean when it's high tide;
Let me help you unburden this feeling of lonesome;
I've been where you're anchored, let me be by your side.

I'll be by your side.

Footnote: Marian's Song is on Sean's albums Rising Tide and The Best of Sean Tyrrell. It's also on YouTube.

56

Home Truths From Afar

THOMAS WOLFE'S books *Look Homeward Angel*, *Of Time and the River* and *You Can't Go Home Again* had a profound effect on me when I studied at ETSU under Professor David McClellan, a wonderful teacher who made the printed page come alive in the classroom and introduced me to giants of American literature like Wolfe, Ernest Hemingway, James Agee, William Faulkner and Jack Kerouac.

It was the richness of Wolfe's prose that held me in thrall. The opening paragraph of *Look Homeward Angel*, a tome of a book, sucked me in and touched me, heart and soul.

In that opening paragraph Wolfe wrote: 'A destiny that leads the English to the Dutch is strange enough; but one that leads from Epsom into Pennsylvania, and thence into the hills that shut in Altamont over the proud coral cry of the cock, and the soft stone smile of an angel, is touched by that dark miracle of chance which makes new magic in a dusty world.'

That first novel of Wolfe was, like all of his fiction, largely autobiographical and had a special pulse for me.

Wolfe grew up in Asheville, North Carolina, only a hundred miles over the highway from Johnson City. A giant of a man who wrote giant-sized books, he died at the tragically young age of 37, but no writer of his generation had his command of language, passion, energy and appetite for life.

Look Homeward Angel is the epic story of Eugene Gant, a brilliant and restless young man whose hunger for intellectual freedom and growth shapes his adolescent years in and around Asheville.

In the book we get to know the incomparable Gant family, including the eccentric and alcoholic stonecutter father and the grasping mother, preoccupied with acquiring real estate, as well as a range of relatives and neighbours all infused with tremendous force and colour.

Written mostly in New York, it brought Wolfe the fame he sought as a writer but it also brought the censure of his neighbours back home in Asheville, many of them outraged at how they had been depicted.

David McClellan's lectures on Wolfe were riveting; it was as if he had brought the author himself into the classroom to talk to us.

Because Wolfe was a lonesome traveller I identified with much of what he wrote, and in particular the vivid and detailed account of the death at a young age of Ben Gant, which is also of course an account of the death of Wolfe's own brother Ben.

My fascination with that passage, was, I believe rooted in an event from childhood that haunted me for many years — the death of my baby brother, Gerard, who was born at home and survived only a couple of days.

I was six at the time and Gerard's death had a deep and lasting effect, compounded I believe by the fact that once he was buried there was nothing further said about Gerard — somehow it felt to me as if he had not mattered at all. I am sure my parents spoke together about their shared loss, but they did not include me in any of those conversations.

For a long time I could not shake off the vision of the small white coffin being carried down the stairs and taken from the house to the local cemetery. To this day I do not know where in the cemetery little Gerard Greally lies, nor did my parents ever reveal the burial place of my sister, who died as a baby before I was born.

For years I would remember the soft cries of my little brother upstairs in the hours after he was born and later the stillness broken only by my mother's wailing.

I understood when in *Look Homeward Angel* Eugene Gant talked of his brother's death and said, 'We can believe in the nothingness of life, we can believe in the nothingness of death and of life after death — but who can believe in the nothingness of Ben?'

William Faulkner, another writer from the deep South, said Thomas Wolfe tried to 'put the whole history of the human heart on the head of a pin'.

In *You Can't Go Home Again* Wolfe tells the story of George Weber, who writes his first book and subsequently travels in New York, London, Paris and Berlin. Weber, just like Eugene Gant, cannot now return; he can't go back home to childhood, to romantic love, to the parents he has lost or has been looking for all his life, to his idealistic younger dreams of glory and fame; he can't go home again to the old forms and systems of things that once seemed permanent but are now in constant flux.

When I read and reread Wolfe's magical prose in *You Can't Go Home Again* I was back in the warm but dysfunctional environment of the home I had left in Ballyhaunis, the place I started from. And I could identify with every word of a lovely passage that spoke Wolfe's own longing for home:

'The way the sunlight came and went upon a certain day, the way grass felt between bare toes, the immediacy of noon, the slamming of an iron gate, the liquid sound of shoe leather on pavements as men came home to lunch, the smell of turnip greens, the clang of ice tongs and the clucking of a hen...Not only these, but all lost sounds and voices, forgotten memories exhumed with a constant pulsing of the brain's great ventricle, until I lived them in my dreams...Nothing had ever been lost.

'All through the ghostly stillness of the land, the train made on forever its tremendous noise, fused of a thousand sounds, and they called back to him forgotten memories...He heard again, as he had heard through his childhood, the pounding wheel, the tolling bell, the whistle-wail, and he remembered how these sounds, coming to him from the river's edge in the little town of his boyhood, had always evoked for him their tongueless prophecy of wild and secret joy, their glorious promises of new lands, morning and a shining city.'

Thomas Wolfe's writings captured my very heart and soul; right away I wanted more than anything else to become a great writer. I was even prepared to shelve my running ambitions in pursuit of the dreams fuelled by David McClellan and Thomas Wolfe.

Years later I would feel I had failed badly on both fronts, and that brought its own deep-set problems that took a long time to solve.

57

Balm On Deep Wounds

I COULD identify and understand when another favourite American author, Pat Conroy, penned what he called *A Love Letter to Thomas Wolfe*, whose writings he had encountered in college in 1961, just over a decade before David McClellan introduced me to the giant from North Carolina.

Conroy's response to his first reading of *Look Homeward Angel* echoed uncannily my own:

'The book itself took full possession of me in a way no book has before or since. I read it from cover to cover three straight times, transfixed by the mesmerising hold of the narrator's voice as I took in and fed on the power of the long line. It was the first time I realised that breathing and the written word were intimately connected to each other. I stepped into the bracing streams of Thomas Wolfe and I could already hear the waterfalls forming in the cliffs that lay invisible beyond me.

'I kept holding my breath as I read *Look Homeward Angel*. The beauty of the language shaped in sentences as pretty as blue herons brought me to my knees with pleasure. I did not know that words could pour through me like honey through a burst hive or that gardens seeded in dark secrecy could bloom along the borders of my half-ruined boyhood because a writer could touch me in all the broken places with his art.'

I learned to appreciate other great American writers during my time at ETSU, but none came close to touching me as deeply as Wolfe. And when during my first summer in Johnson City, David McClellan took me to visit the boarding house in Asheville where

Wolfe grew up and *Look Homeward Angel* was set, I felt I was retracing very step of the writer's youth. Each room in the house now preserved as a memorial to Wolfe was exactly as he described it.

That day in Asheville, when we looked into the room where Wolfe's brother Ben had died, I broke down and poured out my heart to my teacher about the death of my own brother. I told how I watched my parents struggle in different ways with their grief and how a while later, when her sister Eileen died suddenly, my mother started to go around unwashed and dishevelled and how my father would arrive home from work and sit for hours in silence with his eyes closed.

I had never spoken to anyone about those feelings, but I felt that David McClellan would understand.

When my little brother died, my brother Tom had come home from St Jarlath's College in Tuam for a few days and was a great comfort to me. But I was devastated when he left again; it was as if he had abandoned me in a sea of depression with no-one else to talk to.

And so when I read about the death of Ben Gant in *Look Homeward Angel* I was back in the small kitchen in Devlis listening to the doctor tell my father there was nothing more he could do to save Gerard and watching my dad fall apart, overwhelmed by sadness and despair.

I took some solace when I read about the death of Ben Gant and the reaction of his family: 'They were tired, but all felt an enormous relief. For over a day, each had known that death was inevitable and after the horror of the incessant strangling gasp, this peace, this end of pain touched them all with a profound, a weary joy.

'Eugene thought of death now, with love, with joy. Death was like a lovely and tender woman. Ben's friend and lover who had come to free him, to heal him, to save him from the torture of life.

'They stood together without speaking, in Eliza's littered

kitchen, and their eyes were blind with tears, because they thought of lovely and delicate death, and because they loved one another.'

There was something beautifully poignant in Wolfe's evocation of Eugene Gant's feelings in the immediate aftermath: 'Eugene and Luke went softly up the hall and out into the dark. Gently, they closed the big front door behind them and descended the veranda steps. In that enormous silence, birds were waking. It was a little after four o'clock in the morning. Wind pressed the boughs. It was still dark. But above them the thick clouds that had covered the earth for days with a dreary grey blanket had been torn open. Eugene looked up through the deep, ragged vault of the sky and the proud and splendid stars, bright and unwinking. The withered leaves were shaking.

'A cock crew his shrill morning cry of life beginning and awaking. The cock that crew at midnight (thought Eugene) had an elfin ghostly cry. His crow was drugged with sleep and death; it was like a far horn sounding undersea; and it was a warning to all men who are about to die, and to the ghosts that must go home.

'But the cock that crows at morning (he thought) has a voice as shrill as any fife. It says we are done with sleep. We are done with death. O waken, waken into life, says his voice as shrill as any fife. In that enormous silence, birds were waking.

'He heard the cock's bright minstrelsy again, and by the river in the dark the great thunder of flanged wheels, and the long retreating wail of the whistle. And slowly, up the chill deserted street, he heard the heavy ringing clangor of shod hoofs. In that enormous silence, life was waking.'

I found much comfort in reading Thomas Wolfe and I found parallels between the Gant family and my father's family, some of whom were undoubtedly eccentric. I never knew my father's parents, but stories I heard suggested he had grown up in a house not much unlike the Gants'.

I read and reread dozens of the pure prose poems that punctuated Wolfe's writing, passages such as his description of October:

'October is the richest of the seasons. The fields are cut, the granaries are full. The bins are loaded to the brim with fatness. And from the cider-press the rich brown oozing of the York Imperials runs. The bee bores into the belly of the yellowed grape. The fly get old and fat and blue. He buzzes loud, crawls slow, creeps heavily to death on sill and ceiling. The sun goes down in blood and pollen across the bronzed and mown fields of old October.'

Such passages made me feel restless and alive — as if Wolfe had written especially with me in mind. His books became my comfort blanket. They also offered rays of hope on days and nights when the black dogs of depression came barking.

58

Rare And Noble Spirit

LOUIS KENNY called me in late September 2015 with the sad news that my great friend and kindred spirit Robert J 'Jack' Higgs, age 83, had died in Johnson City, Tennessee.

Louis now lives in Nashville and was in Dublin on a rare visit home to Ireland. He knew how much I cared for my old teacher and mentor, and Louis himself had experienced irreparable loss five years before when his lovely wife, Marcia, died from an aneurism.

Jack Higgs cared deeply and passionately about his friends, and for me he was as close as family. I feel blessed to have had the opportunity to visit Jack and his wife, Reny, in Johnson City on three occasions over the past five years. My son Tomás accompanied me on one of those trips and my son Conor on another, and each formed an instant affection for my dear friends.

What I remember best about Jack Higgs will always be his generous spirit and rare wisdom. In the years when I attended ETSU there were two pillars in my life, both English Literature professors — David McClellan, of whom I have already written, and Jack Higgs — and both uniquely talented teachers as well as gifted writers.

I remember standing in the shadows near the Amphitheatre on campus watching in rapture as Jack Higgs taught his class outdoors, proclaiming the gospel according to Thoreau, Emerson or Faulkner. I was instantly attracted to this wonderful teacher whose spellbinding presentations greatly deepened my appreciation of those stellar figures.

I remember too summer evenings in Tennessee, sitting on the front porch of the Higgs home on Okeechobee Drive, discussing life and literature with Jack from every angle. Years later, it seemed we always picked up where we had left off whenever I visited Johnson City.

Jack was a brilliant teacher, editor and prolific writer of international status. One of his several books, *God in the Stadium: Sports and Religion in America*, was nominated for a Pulitzer prize. His *Laurel and Thorn: The Athlete in American Literature* is another of my favourites.

On my last trip to Johnson City, Jack and Reny organised two special evenings that allowed me to fulfil long-held ambitions to publicly honour Coach Dave Walker and Dave McClellan.

And so we had two well attended events in the Library in downtown Johnson City and I was able to pay a symbolic debt of gratitude to two men who had meant a whole lot to me.

It was also the last time I saw Coach Walker, who since then has also departed this mortal world. After a stormy few years, Coach and I had long ago made peace, and we always had a healthy mutual respect, even when not on the one page.

David McClellan's widow and three daughters were there that night I got up to talk and remember my great teacher, and it felt good to speak from the heart and put on record for them the lasting legacy David had left me through his brilliant teaching.

As for Coach Walker, he was visibly surprised and touched by the tribute I delivered — not only on my own behalf but also on behalf of all of the Irish athletes who over many years had gone on scholarship to ETSU.

Jack Higgs loved to talk about his father and I felt that while I never met him, I too knew Bob Higgs well.

Jack was proud of his own considerable academic and sporting achievements — he had played baseball and football — and often talked about the sacrifices his parents made to enable him pursue his education all the way to the US Naval Academy in Annapolis.

There was always a lovely tenderness in Jack's smile when he recounted how his parents, Mary Lee and Bob, sold a cow to pay for the trip to their son's graduation.

He also told me the story of how his father had been underwhelmed by the graduation pomp and ceremony as jet fighters zoomed low overhead and cannons fired as the new graduates flung caps in the air.

Jack could hardly contain his excitement as he went to rejoin his parents, eager to hear their reaction to the pyrotechnics, the top brass, the drama and colour of it all.

Mary Lee was of course massively impressed and every bit as excited as her son. But Bob was more grounded, ever mindful of his humble roots in the tiny farming community of Anes Station. And so he put it all into earthy, but profound, Middle-Tennessee perspective.

'Son,' he said in answer to Jack's probing, 'I noticed when they fired them big guns, those pigeons sure did haul ass.'

Jack always laughed heartily when he told me that story.

He and Reny also enjoyed reminding me of another occasion, when I attended a Christmas soiree in their home. The drinks flowed freely and it was well into the night when I excused myself to go to the bathroom. When after half an hour I had not rejoined the party, Jack went in search and found me sleeping like a baby — full length in the bath.

The Higgs residence was always full of welcome and I loved to visit there.

As well as being academically brilliant Jack Higgs was firmly rooted in the soil and never forgot those humble beginnings. As one who believes home is really where you start out from, I always felt that Jack had an eternal longing and love for the place he grew up in. In that way he reminded me very much of my own father.

I welcomed Jack and Reny Higgs to Dublin on one occasion in the mid-1980s and it was my pleasure to introduce Jack to Con

Houlihan, another down-home country man who had followed the literary path to soaring success.

Like Con, Jack Higgs was big in both heart and stature. He was a great friend to all of us Irish athletes at ETSU, and when I met Louis Kenny in Dublin, we talked and remembered with great fondness our dear, departed friend.

Jack always encouraged me to write, and when we'd talk on the phone he would enquire how my long-promised second book was progressing.

He had himself a huge manuscript in constant progress — a fascinating autobiographical tome he seemed reluctant to let go of. I reckon Jack would have wanted me to finish my own story once started, and I would give a lot to be able to send him a copy of the printed work.

As I talked with Louis Kenny, I recalled one of the last conversations I had with Jack Higgs, when, not for the first time, we got to discussing Thomas Wolfe.

There is a passage by Wolfe at the end of *You Can't Go Home Again* that I believe is appropriate to mark Jack Higgs's final journey.

Something has spoken to me in the night, burning the tapers of the waning year; something has spoken to me in the night and told me I shall die, I know not where. Saying: 'To lose the earth you know for greater knowing; to lose the life you have for greater life; to leave the friends you loved for greater loving; to find a land more kind than home, more large than earth — whereon the pillars of the earth are founded, toward which the conscience if the world is tending — a wind is rising, and the rivers flow.'

I could not let this book go down the slipway without including this little tribute to a man whose spirit will always be close to me.

59

Running Full Circle

I HAVE my granddaughter, Hayleigh Bone, and my grandson Thomas Branigan Greally to thank for giving me the prompt to return to regular running and rediscover the lovely sense of play and innocence involved.

As a result of that prompting, my running career came full circle on an August evening of 2015, when I went back to the track in the Morton Stadium and along with family and friends, including seven Olympians, ran for 30 minutes and 17 seconds.

The 30:17 was significant, because it recalled the time I posted exactly 45 years earlier in setting a national junior record for 10,000 metres — a record that remains intact. Four and a half decades on, I covered 4,950 metres on what was a night, Tuesday August 18, of very special celebration and gratitude.

Hayleigh Bone is six and loves nothing better than to race like the wind around a special spot in Rialto she calls 'The Circle Field'. It's about two years since I started to bring Hayleigh to that little green oasis hard by the Grand Canal, but back then I was content to just watch my first grandchild joyfully stride out.

Then one day she posed a searching question: 'My mam (Catherine) said you used to be a runner — why do you not run now?'

That was when a light went on again for me and I resolved not to be a spectator anymore — it was past time I made a sustained attempt to get back in harness. There had been so many starts and stutters over so many years and so many broken promises I had made to myself to get fully fit again.

Marian Finucane had played a part in keeping me going, when having read a piece I had written in the *Irish Runner Yearbook* she twice had me as a guest on her Saturday radio show on RTÉ. Sharing my 'return to running' story motivated me and also seemed to resonate with listeners, a good few of whom phoned or emailed me afterwards.

It was, however, David Carrie, *Irish Runner* columnist and charismatic leader of Team Carrie in Dunleer, who provided the definitive prompt.

David had for five years been training groups of 150 locals, of all ages and abilities, to run the Dublin Marathon — extraordinary when you consider the population of Dunleer is roughly 2,500.

I had brave intentions of joining up with Team Carrie and made a few forays to their sessions but, sadly, repeated the same old story, allowing work and other distractions to derail the effort.

Not long after young Hayleigh put the hard question, Carrie came calling with a question of his own: 'What are you going to do, Frank, to celebrate the 45th anniversary of your junior 10,000m record?'

Without waiting for my answer, he came back with his own: 'I think it's time you knuckled down and committed to a training plan that can get you back running. I suggest you return to Santry in August and celebrate with a sustained run for those 30 minutes and 17 seconds.'

David continued, 'I know you tried to get back running last year, but I also noticed that you tried to do too much too soon, and how that early overload dampened your enthusiasm.'

I promised David an answer in a few days' time — and when I next went to The Circle Field with Hayleigh Bone and Thomas Branigan Greally I was dressed to run.

If I was still prevaricating about the Santry retrospective, David forced the issue when in front of 200 members of Team Carrie at a Dublin Marathon Celebration Dinner in the Grove Hotel in Dunleer he announced that a certain Frank Greally would be running in a special event in the Morton Stadium in August 2015.

That final challenge by David set me off on a 10-month odyssey that gave me a whole new lease of life at age 64.

Starting in late 2014, I followed a training plan devised by David Carrie and Catherina McKiernan and for once I listened to advice, starting with a walk-jog-run programme (walk for three minutes, jog for a minute) and gradually progressing over several weeks until I could run continuously for over 40 minutes.

I was greatly helped through the months by several people. My good friend Ray McManus of Sportsfile tracked my progress. The pedicurist Peter Winner looked after my feet and massage. And Rob and Emma of Gourmet Fuel cooked up nutritious meals aimed at weight loss and increased vitality.

Aidan Woods, Olympic Physiotherapist, rowed in, as did another long-time friend, the physical therapist Gerard Hartmann. All my work colleagues at Athletics Ireland were hugely supportive, especially our CEO, John Foley.

My wife, Marian, and children — Tomás, Catherine, Conor, Laura and Claire — were a constant source of incentive and encouragement as, with my friend Feidhlim Kelly riding shotgun, I bought into the training regime.

I called the event in Santry my Gratitude Run — gratitude for the freedom and opportunities and every bit of sweetness I have known during a life to which running has always been central.

Ronnie Delany did me the signal honour of acting as official starter, and my boyhood hero the ageless and unstoppable Ron Hill was a special guest.

Other legends such as Dessie McGann, John Treacy, Neil Cusack, Catherina McKiernan and Fionnuala Britton committed to running a few laps with me on a night that will long linger in the memory.

To make it all extra sweet, I was joined on a lap by little Hayleigh Bone, and it gladdened my heart to see her racing ahead of me, striding out beautifully, so innocent and free, down the home straight.

My two grandsons sons, Thomas and Luke Branigan Greally, were also full of running on the night, and it was heartening to see lots of other youngsters enjoying themselves.

The paced miles, open to runners of all abilities, were hugely popular, and my youngest daughter, Claire, made her track debut, clocking just over nine minutes.

To complete a rare and wonderful evening, my sons, Tomás and Conor, joined me for the last lap and my daughters Catherine and Laura gave me massive vocal support.

Neil Cusack was there, as was another member of our collegiate squad in Tennessee, Ray McBride. Ray was the life and soul of the Irish Brigade, and the most versatile, an extravagantly gifted runner, dancer, musician, writer and actor who after returning home starred in roles for stage, cinema and TV.

He was an Ireland and world step-dancing champion, and a clip on YouTube still shows him performing on RTÉ's *The Late Late Show* — those brilliant feet tapping out their playful rhythms well ahead of the Riverdance era.

Then over a decade ago, Ray was struck down by a cancer that affected his speech and balance. For a force of nature such as Ray, it was a savage blow. And yet I have never heard my great friend complain about the cards he was dealt.

I dedicated my Gratitude Run to Ray — the evening raised funds for specialist IT equipment and training to allow him reconnect on the internet with his many friends at home and abroad.

There was a particularly poignant moment for Neil and myself when at Ray's bidding we ran a lap of the track, pushing him in his wheelchair.

I thought of all of the great days we three had shared running in the hills of Tennessee. I thought too of how our real wealth is our health. Of the three of us, Ray drew the short straw in the health stakes and I was very mindful of that on the night.

If I have a message to impart here, it is simply that it is never too late to return to running. When I started back training, I felt like a rusty machine that had been left out too long in the rain. This time around, though, I listened to the wise counsel of David and Catherina and Feidhlim as they coaxed me to incremental improvements not only of body but also of mind.

I would say to anyone of my age who has grandchildren, don't settle for just watching your grandchildren run — get fit and run with them and discover again the magic of playful running.

It reminds me of a line from my great friend Dr George Sheehan, the late and original Running Guru: 'What most runners have in their daily run is a special place for mental and spiritual life. But it comes with easy running, at a pace that frees the mind to create and the spirit to soar.'

George encouraged runners to recapture that sense of play we all experienced in the schoolyard. 'Play is an expression of the true self,' he said, 'the person the Creator had in mind the day we were born.'

Sheehan also liked to quote the English social scientist Walter Bagehot: 'Man made the school; God made the schoolyard.' A powerful message for all educators.

Some days are diamonds and in the Morton Stadium in Santry on that August evening I felt I had somehow come full circle in a life that has had many bumps and scrapes along the way.

When I look back over all the years, I am grateful to be still standing, and like Willie Nelson, 'after taking several readings, I'm surprised to find my mind's still fairly sound.'

And when I think of old Willie, I also think of Kris Kristofferson and another great song, *This Old Road*:

'Look at that old photograph, is it really you/ Smiling like a baby full of dreams/ Smiling's not so easy now/ Some are coming through/ Nothing's as simple as it seems/ But I guess you find your blessings/ In the problems that you're dealing with today/ Like the changing of the seasons/ Ain't you come a long way/ Ain't you come a long way down this old road.'

That old road sure took a lot of twists and turns since I set out all those years ago from the little house in Devlis, Ballyhaunis. If I feel anything right now it's truly blessed and grateful to have the love of family and many terrific friends whose support is constant.

Afterword

I HAVE come to believe running is as much a spiritual experience as a physical one, and the older I get the more convinced I become.

I am convinced that at difficult times of my life, many of which I have charted in these pages, my running background sustained me — even if I was doing absolutely no running during the term of trial in question.

I have over the years heard many others echo the belief, describing how running lifted their spirits through episodes of sadness, depression or recovery from illness.

Most runners have experienced and embraced some physical pain in training and racing, but the feeling of wellbeing that inevitably ensues more than compensates for the discomfort.

The act of running is creative too, and the late Dr George Sheehan referred to his running as 'the hub in the centre of my life'. That metaphor I am sure will strike a chord with many of us who run.

For a number of reasons, while writing this book I have been thinking about George Sheehan. The waning year conjures memories of running with George and Noel Carroll and another great pal, JP Murray, through the splendour of County Wicklow's Djouce Woods on a bright October Saturday morning and afterwards spending a couple of carefree hours in a little café in Bray chatting about running and life.

Now I am back in full stride I often think while out running about my Irish Brigade comrades and wonder how they are doing.

When we were all together in Tennessee people reckoned Ray McBride, Neil Cusack and myself were the most likely of the Irish to put down roots there. It transpired to the contrary; it was Eddie Leddy, Ray Flynn, Louis Kenny, Kevin Breen and Tom McCormack who made permanent homes in the USA and went on to prosper in their chosen professions.

While writing this book I received a phone call from Tom McCormack and he reminded me of a summer in Johnson City when we had no work and learned on a few occasion the hard reality of hunger knock.

We spent those few months in a dormitory and between us we had just a couple of cassette tapes, one of Gordon Lightfoot and one of Cat Stevens — since which a Gordon Lightfoot song never fails to trigger fond recollections of those tough days.

Tom recalled how when starvation threatened we came up with a stratagem to keep body and soul together — we would masquerade as workers at the College Grill, where we had washed dishes during term.

Every evening we entered the grill by the back door and went upstairs through the kitchen, grabbing aprons to suggest we had just finished a shift. We would make a big play of depositing those aprons in the bin upstairs while calling out to Nora, the elderly manageress, to throw on a couple of double burgers and plenty of French fries. I suspected Nora knew well that we were chancing our arm, but that kindly lady fed us throughout that summer.

Tom McCormack also reminded me that I had been short only a very few credits, in Maths and Science, to graduate at ETSU, but I could never knuckle down to those subjects — and that has been one of my regrets.

I have always been good at bringing people together, and five years ago when Tomás and I visited Johnson City, I managed with the help of Ray Flynn to organise an Irish Brigade reunion of sorts — a party hosted my Ray in his impressive residence just outside the city.

Eddie Leddy, Tom McCormack and Louis Kenny were there, as was Coach Walker himself, and we had great reminiscing and great fun as we talked about old times.

Marcia Kenny was there too. Whenever on visits Stateside I had stayed over with Louis and Marcia, she had always been hugely supportive. We had walked and talked about family and friends and literature, and I little thought that meeting at Ray's place would be our last.

Tomás and I were barely home when we got word of Marcia's sudden death from an aneurism. A poem I wrote in her memory includes these lines: *'We were walking, talking on a day in May/ Through Johnson City, you had much to say/ It's family that matters most, you said/ Your words still echo in my head.'*

That core family value came full circle for me in 2014 with a welcome return to running, a first family wedding and a visit from my brother, Tom, who made it home from Australia for the big celebration.

The highlight of that admittedly wobbly running year was striding out happily along a scenic trail on the stunningly beautiful Inish Beg Estate in West Cork on the morning of Conor's wedding to Tracey Wade.

That run on a bright, heaven-sent morning will long remain a cherished memory. And the memory of a day and evening when everything seemed to come together for us as a family will sustain me for whatever time I have left on the planet.

I never reached the Olympian heights I might have as an athlete and my story is not one of world records or championship medals. It is more a tale of survival and I think some of the hundreds of Irish athletes lucky enough and talented enough to win US scholarships may empathise.

There were, no doubt, many Irish athletes who, like me, 'fell through the cracks' in America — to borrow from the poet AE Housman, 'runners whom renown outran and the name died before the man'.

And so I cherish my life today and the good health and ability to still be able to put one foot in front of the other, whether on trails in the Phoenix Park or in our little Circle Field by the canal.

And I know now that Hayleigh Bone will never again have to put the hard question: 'Grandad, why do you not run anymore?'

I'm too grateful now to ever stop running.

Index